D. J. Collinson

Writing English

A workbook for students

Pan Books London and Sydney

D. J. Collinson is a staff tutor and senior lecturer in philosophy at the Open University.

First published 1982 by Pan Books Ltd,
Cavaye Place, London SW10 9PG
2nd printing 1983
© D. J. Collinson 1982
ISBN 0 330 26584 9
Filmset by Northumberland Press Ltd, Gateshead, Tyne and Wear
Printed in Great Britain by Collins, Glasgow

for D. W. C.

Acknowledgements

I am very grateful to those who were kind enough to
read and comment on the first draft of this book:
David Roberts, Keith Dockray, Gill Kay, Kathleen O'Connor,
D. J. O'Connor, Ellen Petrie, Neil Richards, and Ben Collinson;
and also to Maggie Ovenden for typing the drafts, and to Edgar
Russell for reading the proofs.

Contents

part three: Answers to Exercises

Introduction

Writing English is for students of all ages who want to improve their written work and present it in the best possible way. In writing this book I have had in mind people working in sixth forms, in colleges, and those starting degree courses.

The book has two main parts. Part One concentrates on spelling, punctuation, and grammar: the basic requirements of lucid writing. Part Two deals with a range of writing techniques: essay-writing, note-taking, style and diction, examination work, and the use of special terms and conventions required for the presentation of essays, articles, dissertations, and projects.

The first chapter takes the form of a quiz requiring the identification of some common failings in writing English – errors of spelling, punctuation, grammar, style, and meaning. Thereafter the chapters deal systematically with those kinds of failing. There are exercises throughout, and answers to the exercises are given in Part Three. Each chapter is arranged in six sections so as to offer a programme of work that does not encroach too noticeably on routine study time. A section takes about fifteen or twenty minutes to complete, and so may be worked in a coffee break or on a short bus or train journey. Someone working at the rate of one section a day would complete the book in about six weeks.

I have a few suggestions for anyone who decides to work through the exercises. First, use a dictionary when it is recommended, and resist the temptation to look up the answers before completing an exercise. Second, be critically alert to everything you read, from advertisements to text books, to see if it is clear and concise in a way that is appropriate to it. Third, try to talk to friends, other students or your family about what you are doing in the book. They may enjoy helping with the exercises and discussing the topics, and this kind of additional interest can only increase your own understanding and mastery of the material.

It is not essential to work through *Writing English* systematically, especially if there are one or two particular topics you are keen to get to grips with immediately. The book's scope is fairly wide, ranging from the rudiments of writing learned in the early years of secondary school to the details of how to write footnotes and bibliographies; so you may well find yourself able to work more quickly on some chapters than on others. Your performance in the opening spot-the-mistake chapter will give some indication of which chapters will be especially useful to you, and a quick look at the revision exercises at the end of each chapter should give a good idea of the detailed topics covered in the chapters. There is a Bibliography at the end of Part Two and a comprehensive Index at the end of the book.

You shouldn't expect to acquire from the book an absolutely rigid and unequivocal set of rules for good writing and presentation. A language is as lively as the people who use and make it; it is something that develops and changes, and with it the rules and conventions for its written forms. But such changes come about gradually and there is always a core of common practice that has general acceptance and understanding. This book is about that common practice: it offers guidelines to some of the established usages, rules and conventions of written English.

part one:
Basics

1 Spot the mistakes

Below are twenty examples of incorrect, sloppy, or thought-less English. For each example please do three things:

- encircle the faulty word or words;
- briefly describe what is wrong;
- try to write a correct or improved version.

Describing exactly what is wrong can be difficult, but there is no need to give full, technical descriptions of the mistakes. It is quite enough to say such things as 'grammar wrong', 'meaning confused', 'punctuation wrong', 'spelling wrong', 'wordy', and so on.

1

She was definately finding it difficult to keep up with the others.

fault

correction

2

The locomotive has it's own reserve power supply.

fault

correction

3

When the obsession with deafening rock music is over.

fault

correction

4

The investment yielded an annual income of five hundred pounds a year.

fault

correction

5

We have been cognisant of the nature of this problem over a period of the order of a decade.

fault

correction

6

I have now discussed the proposal for restocking all the deep freezers with my colleagues.

fault

correction

7

The committee has not announced their decision yet.

fault

correction

8

It is esential to spell correctly.

fault

correction

9

The president of the society, acting on medical advice, has resigned his office, and we have no alternative but to accept it.

fault

correction

10

The owner of a piece of equipment, which does not comply with these regulations, is liable to a fine or imprisonment.

fault

correction

11

Add distilled water until there is five cubic centimetres of liquid in the test tube.

fault

correction

12

His illness can only be alleviated by drugs.

fault

correction

13

The cause of the hold-up on the production-line was due to a fault in the conveyor-belt.

fault

correction

14

The seminar ended by an open discussion.

fault

correction

15

The drug produced unpleasant side-effects in a percentage of cases.

fault

correction

16

There have been two magnificent victories for the British teams today, and they have won both of them.

fault

correction

17

Many birds are now protected species, i.e. the osprey, the bittern, the golden eagle, the buzzard.

fault

correction

18

He complained about the teaching, and then said he was completely disinterested in the subject anyway.

fault

correction

19

He literally made mincemeat of his opponent.

fault

correction

20

Before they arrived at the meeting they had already prepared their replies in advance.

fault

correction

My corrections are on pp. 169–72.

2 Spelling

Some people seem to have no trouble with spelling; others have to work hard at it. Those who find it easy generally have a natural ability to picture words mentally: they can see the 'look' of a word in the mind's eye. Those who find spelling difficult, and who do not naturally do much remembering and thinking with mental 'photographs', can try to develop that ability. But there are other ways of overcoming the difficulties.

You will need your dictionary to hand for this chapter.

Improve your spelling

Here are a few ways of improving your spelling:

● Keep a dictionary to hand when you are writing, and look up any words concerning which you have even the slightest doubt.

● To learn a difficult word, try picturing it printed large in a bright colour.

● Invent a rhyme or phrase to help you remember a tricky

spelling: 'possesses possesses five s's' is a well-known one.

- Learn some of the basic rules of spelling. (We shall be looking at a few of them in this chapter.)
- Make a list of the words you regularly find troublesome. Take one word at a time, write it on a card, and put the card where you will see it often. Break the word into sections and underline the section that causes all the trouble, e.g. MIS/<u>CHIEV</u>/OUS. The simple act of writing or printing a word correctly two or three times is very helpful.

Exercise 1

Fill the gaps in the following words:

ac _ om _ odate	deteri__rate
vac _ in _ te	Feb _ uary
com _ i _ ted	i _ oculate
partic_l__ly	para__el
ar _ tic	ac _ ess
contemp _ rary	sep _ r _ te
mis _ ellan _ ous	vet _ _ inary
recu _ rence	reco _ nise

Check your spellings by looking the words up in your dictionary.

Answers for Chapter 2 are on pp. 172–9.

Exercise 2

Underline and correct any wrong spellings in the sentences below. Use your dictionary if necessary:

1 The Glorious Revolution of seventeenth-century England has always held a facination for me.
2 Cyclonic conditions usually bring changable weather to the Cornish peninsula.

3 The chief laboratory assistant was disatisfied with the penicillen samples and ordered a different culture for the repeat of the experiment.
4 The vallies below volcanos are particularly rich in alluvial soil.
5 When the commando force moved forward, all the armoured cars remained stationery, as the order to procede with the manouevre was inaudable to the drivers.
6 There is a noticably transcendant quality in the work of many of our contempory painters.

Exercise 3

This exercise tests again your spelling of some of the words in exercises 1 and 2. Fill the gaps in the following sentences:

1 The injured dog was taken immediately to a v_____y surgeon.
2 Candlemas is a festival of very early spring and is celebrated in the first week of F_____y.
3 It is impossible for p_____l lines to meet or intersect.
4. Cream kept for more than a couple of days, even in a refrigerator, will begin to d_____e.
5 Is immunity to diphtheria given by v_____n or i_____n?
6 I am p_____y interested in the biographies of those explorers who have been to the a_____c.
7 Only three years ago she was a c_____y of mine in the sixth form, but today I didn't r_____e her.

Take a good hard look at the following words. They are all spelt correctly:

diphtheria	successful	occasionally
exaggerate	abbreviation	develop
omission	committee	ascertain

Choose a word you find difficult to spell, write it on a card, and put the card where you will see it often, e.g.

suc/cess/ful

If you looked up *recognise* in your dictionary when you did exercise 1, you probably noticed that it may end in either -*ise* or -*ize*. Be cautious in your use of -*ize* endings for words of this sort. There are some English words that must have the -*ise* ending (despise, enterprise, exercise, comprise, improvise, and many others), so if in doubt use -*ise* (except for prize) and you will not then be at fault.

Two spelling rules

The trouble with most spelling rules is that they are rather complicated, are difficult to remember, and have long lists of exceptions. On the whole it is better to learn individual difficult spellings than an elaborate rule and its exceptions. But there are just a few rules that are straightforward, very useful, and quite easy to remember. We shall look at two of them in this section.

Most of us know the following rule:

When the sound rhymes with 'bee'
Put i before e
Except after c

An exception to that rule is *seize*: it has the 'ee' sound that rhymes with bee, it has no 'c' in front, and yet it is spelt 'ei'. If you pronounce *neither* and *either* with the long 'ee' sound, then I suppose that they too should be counted as exceptions.

Exercise 4

Fill in the blanks in the sentences below, using the rule above to guide you, and referring to a dictionary if necessary:

1 It is better to give than to rec __ ve.
2 An escutcheon is a sh __ ld, or sh __ ld-shaped object.

22

3 Michelangelo had to be suspended in a kind of hammock in order to paint the c __ ling of the Sistine Chapel.

4 The practised woodman can w __ ld an axe with marvellous accuracy.

5 He had the knack of perc __ ving the very thing I wished to conceal or disguise.

6 I have no idea of the details of what happened at the rel __ f of Mafeking.

7 The prairie lands of the mid-West of the USA are renowned for their magnificent y __ lds of hard wheat.

8 I like the sort of dog that will go bounding into the sea to retr __ ve a stick or ball.

9 How he came to lose his passport from his inner pocket is quite inconc __ vable.

10 We are not quite sure how to tell him that we all object to his conc __ ted attitude.

The second rule concerns suffixes. A suffix is a syllable added to the end of a word, e.g. *-ly* in *nicely*.

A suffix added to a word that ends with a silent 'e' does not change the word spelling if the suffix starts with a consonant. It does change the spelling if the suffix starts with a vowel. Thus:

● if *amuse* is given the consonant-suffix *-ment* it becomes *amusement;*

● if given the vowel-suffix *-ing* it becomes *amusing* (the silent 'e' is dropped).

In spite of some exceptions (e.g. mileage, ageing, changeable) this is an extremely useful rule.

Exercise 5

Fill the gaps in the sentences below by adding the appropriate suffix (*-ing*, *-ment*, *-ation*, or *-ed*) to the word given in brackets at the beginning of each sentence:

1 (advertise) He has been _____ for new staff for the past three weeks.
2 (recognise) Both felt that after twenty-five years _____ one another might be difficult.
3 (encourage) Nearly all the children diagnosed as 'insecure' improved greatly once they were given _____.
4 (explore) My thesis will consist mainly of an _____ of the social relations of the small island community from which I collected all my data.
5 (arrange) Part of her research time will have to be given to _____ the duke's letters in chronological order.
6 (compete) He hopes to be _____ in the 1984 Olympic Games in Los Angeles.
7 (devastate) The paper described his election defeat as 'a _____ blow to his political career'.

Exercise 6

Underline and correct the misspelt words in the following passage. Most of them are words already used in this chapter, but a few are new:

One day in Februay last year, whilst practicing my clarinet, I became victim of an unfortunate event. Without warning, the cieling of my study fell, devastateing the careful arrangment of my books, music, and personal posessions that I had completed only the day before.

Strangely enough, this event was the fulfillment of a prophesy made by my sister when she visited me earlier that week. She had pointed out some obvious signs of deterioration in the cieling's plasterwork, had peered at the ocasional white flake on the table surface, and noted other small omens of iminent collapse. At the time I dissmissed all this as exageration, thinking she was perhaps a little envious of the independant and successfull life I had begun to lead once I had seperated myself from the rest of the family, and so had siezed the first opportunity to genarate a little anxiety in my life. But to be fair to her, she was apalled when she subsequently learned she had indeed been a phrophet of doom. Little did she know, when she offered to help put things right, that she was to be

one of the principle characters in the fasinating and frightening
events that were to ensue.

Latin and Greek plurals; similar words

Many Latin and Greek words have become incorporated
into the English language, and the spelling of some of them,
in particular of their plural forms, can cause difficulty. This
is mainly because their plurals are not formed by adding an
's' or an 'es', as so many English plurals are, and so they tend
not to 'look' plural to us.

Exercise 7

Below are listed the plurals of some commonly used Latin
and Greek words. Try writing their *singulars*, which in most
cases are better-known than the plurals. Use your dictionary
to learn any meanings and spellings with which you are not
familiar:

appendices
crises
data
criteria
phenomena
errata
indices
bacteria
maxima
memoranda
media
parentheses
stimuli
strata
formulae

Exercise 8

Complete the unfinished words in the sentences below:

1 We use the term 'unidentified flying objects' to refer to all those inexplicable phenomen _____ that appear from time to time in the sky.

2 The book has a bibliography, copious footnotes, and two appendi _____.

3 A criteri____ is a kind of standard or yardstick for making judgements.

4 A memorand _____ urging strict economy has been sent to every department and office in the building.

5 The word 'dat _____' refers to a number of items of information; 'dat _____' refers to just one such item.

6 A series of minor cris _____ preceded the serious breakdown of efficiency at the shipyard.

7 The proof-reading of the book was so badly done that we are having to supply a long list of errat _____.

8 A bacteri _____ is visible only under a very powerful microscope.

Sometimes a word gets spelt wrongly because it is confused with a similar word. Read through the pairs of words below, thinking about their meanings, and look up any of which you are uncertain:

principle principal	practice practise
stationery stationary	advice advise
compliment complement	prophecy prophesy
affect effect	device devise
	dependent dependant

(Note: some dictionaries give *dependent* and *dependant* as interchangeable, but it is accepted practice to use depend*ant* for the person who is depend*ent* upon someone or something else.)

Exercise 9

In the sentences below, underline the correct word in each pair:

1 'Always tell the truth' is an example of a moral principal/principle.
2 It isn't difficult to imagine what kind of affect/effect long-term unemployment can have on a person.
3 Practice/practise makes perfect.
4 A stationer sells stationery/stationary.
5 If his prophesy/prophecy about the end of the world is fulfilled next week, he won't even be able to say 'I told you so'.
6 Is it true that almost anyone with a physics degree is capable of making a nuclear devise/device?
7 If she really is financially dependent/dependant on him, then the document is correct in citing her as one of his dependants/dependents.
8 I need some expert advice/advise on the whole business of job applications and interviews.
9 The compliment/complement of the order is being sent immediately.

The apostrophe

An apostrophe is a sign like a raised comma. It has two main uses:

- to denote possession: 'the dog's tail' (the tail *of the dog*);
- to show that a letter has been omitted: 'isn't' (is n*o*t).

Understanding when and how to use the apostrophe is a matter of grammar as well as of spelling. In this section we shall look at its uses and the difficulties connected with them.

The apostrophe denoting possession is used only with nouns. A singular noun is followed by 's:

the *girl's* clothes

A plural noun *that ends with an s* is followed by ' only:

the *girls'* clothes

Plural nouns that do not end with s are followed by 's:

the *children's* clothes

Exercise 10
Rewrite the following phrases using the apostrophe to denote possession:

1 the shade of the tree
2 the braying of the ass
3 the education of the princess
4 the boots of the men
5 the damp course of the house
6 the robes of the duchesses
7 the books of Rosemary
8 the careers of the students
9 the losses of the armies
10 the discussions of the women

Difficulties sometimes arise when we want to use the apostrophe with singular nouns that end with *s*, e.g. rhinoceros. To add 's to a word that already ends with *s* produces a sound some people find objectionable:

the rhinoceros's tusks

It has therefore become the practice with some singular nouns that end with *s* to drop the *s* that follows the apostrophe:

the rhinoceros' tusks

There is no fixed rule about this; we may do as we wish. But if the singular noun ending in *s* has only one syllable it is usual to add the whole 's:

28

St James's Street

And even if the singular noun ending in *s* has two or more syllables, provided it is not made unbearably ugly by the addition, it is better to add the whole *'s*:

Pythagoras's theorem
St Thomas's hospital

Sometimes the advice is given to overcome the sort of ugliness produced by 'the rhinoceros's tusks' by circumlocution, that is, by using a phrase such as 'the tusks of the rhinoceros'.

Exercise 11

Rewrite the following phrases using the apostrophe to denote possession:

1 the wanderings of Ulysses
2 the properties of the gas
3 the room of Mr Jones
4 an imprisonment of one year
5 the lair of the hippopotamus
6 the skin of the potato

An occasional use of the apostrophe is to make clear an unusual plural which would not otherwise be clear. For instance, the sentence

There are two is in 'radii'

is not clear until we write:

There are two i's in 'radii'.

This use of the apostrophe is not necessary if the meaning is clear without it, as in

Let us have no more ifs and buts.

The possessive pronouns, *hers*, *yours*, *theirs*, *ours* and *its*, do not require an apostrophe, but the possessive of *one* does:

What happens to one's heavier luggage after it is placed on the conveyor belt?

There are sometimes difficulties connected with *its*. *Its* is a possessive pronoun:

I can't open my case because I've lost its key.

But *its* must not be confused with *it's*. *It's* is not the possessive of *it* but a contraction of *it is*. The apostrophe in *it's* shows that an i has been left out:

It's (it is) now known that bats are carriers of disease.

Exercise 12
Insert apostrophes where necessary in the following sentences:

1 How does a spider make its web?
2 I shall have to remember to dot my is and cross my ts.
3 Do you know where the Joneses live in St Marks Street?
4 The room on the left is yours, that on the right is ours.
5 Please let me know if its convenient for Michaels daughter to use your secretarys room on Thursday evening.
6 St Matthews Gospel has a different character from St Johns.
7 Its not easy to run childrens parties in small houses.
8 He took them into a room which was a collectors paradise.
9 He was sentenced to six years imprisonment.
10 All of this years tomatoes have been spoilt by a fungus

The use of the apostrophe to show that letters have been omitted occurs mainly in the writing of conversations in which words such as *doesn't*, *isn't*, and *can't* are used. It can also indicate the omission of figures:

He owns a splendidly preserved '52 Volkswagen.

Apostrophes are *not* used to form the plurals of abbreviations, initials, and figures. The plural of 1980 is 1980s, of VIP, VIPs. But apostrophes *are* used to form the *possessives* of abbreviations, initials, and figures:

The BBC's programmes for the coming year ...
The MPs' enthusiastic cheering ...
007's hair-raising adventures ...

Exercise 13

Place or remove apostrophes and correct any spelling mistakes where necessary in the following passage:

It isnt easy to say exactly what it was about Henrys life, in those golden days of the 1960's, that made ones own seem so unpromising. Certain diferences were plain. His fathers job meant that Henry was always meeting MPs and famous men, not to mention their daughters. His mothers money guarenteed that he never had to do a days work to support himself. The idea of keeping up with the Joneses' meant nothing to Henry, for his lifes ambition was of another sort. His hearts desires bore no resemblences to yours or mine, for he all ready possessed everything that we might long for only in a dreams insanity.

I cant deny that my life then had it's own glamour. Certainly, at the time, I didnt complain of a lack of exitement. All the Henry's in the world could not diminish my joy in Annes love. Yet I had a sense of oportunities missed; and above all, a sense of the gods disaproval casting it's shadow on the path before me.

Exercise 14

Write the plurals of:

appendix
crisis
index
phenomenon
erratum

Common pitfalls

Spelling difficulties often arise over nouns that describe *people* by reference to their work or to what they do, and *things* by reference to their functions, e.g. actor, painter, generator, transistor. The difficulty with many of these sorts of words is in knowing whether they end with an -*or* or an -*er*. It is sometimes pointed out that, in general, the ending -*or* is found in words for *things*, and the ending -*er* in words for *people*. But there are so many exceptions to this rule that it is scarcely worth remembering.

Exercise 15
Complete the following words with either -*er* or -*or*, using a dictionary if necessary:

govern_____	perpetrat_____	radiat_____
oppress_____	desert_____	garden_____
paint_____	fertilis_____	angl_____
don_____	transmitt_____	confection_____
comput_____	incinerat_____	consum_____
station_____	eras_____	propell_____
decorat_____	promot_____	manufactur_____
abett_____	protect_____	possess_____
purvey_____	conquer_____	credit_____
invent_____	mot_____	prosecut_____

Exercise 16
For each pair of spellings given below, decide which spelling is correct and write it in the third column. Please don't skip the writing-out of the correct spellings; it is an important

part of the activity of learning new spellings and consolidating knowledge you have already:

sovereign	sovreign
proffessor	professor
Meditteranean	Mediterranean
privilege	privelige
aggravate	agravate
embarass	embarrass
disappear	disapear
liesure	leisure
fulfillment	fulfilment
nuisance	nuiscance
battalion	batalion
apalling	appalling
skilfull	skilful

There is one more helpful rule of spelling which, although it has some exceptions, has wide application. It deals with the question whether the final consonant of a word is *doubled* when adding the suffixes -*ed* and -*ing*. For instance, does *get* become *geting* or *getting*?

The rule is as follows. A single final consonant is doubled if the word is pronounced with a short sound, as in *drip*, *yap*, *set*, *thud*; it is not doubled if the word is pronounced with a long sound, as in *meet*, *fail*, *cool*, *smile*:

drip, dripped, dripping	meet, meeting
yap, yapped, yapping	fail, failed, failing
set, setting	cool, cooled, cooling
thud, thudded, thudding	smile, smiled, smiling

Exercise 17
Complete the unfinished words in the sentences below:

1 The butterfly will come to no harm if you carry it in your cup_____ hands.

2 A tumult of clap _____ broke out as he finished his speech.
3 She is researching into the origins of the can _____ industry in the North-east.
4 On a hot day, bees can be seen cool _____ their hive by fan _____ with their wings at its entrance.
5 The geese have crop _____ the grass to a short, even texture.
6 The young cabbage plants are droop _____ from lack of water.

Spelling the plurals of some words can be tricky, simply because there are very few rules. There is, however, a rule for forming the plurals of nouns that end in *y*:

- If the letter before the *y* is a vowel, as in *monkey*, then an *s* is added to form the plural *monkeys;*
- If the letter before the *y* is a consonant, as in *sentry*, then the *y* is changed into an *i* and *es* is added to form the plural *sentries*.

There is no rule for forming the plurals of words ending in an *o*. These plurals have to be learned by trying to picture them in the mind's eye or by inventing jingles that group like words together. The plural of a word ending in *oo* is always formed by adding an *s*.

Exercise 18
Write the plurals of the words listed below, using a dictionary if necessary:

journey	buffalo
kangaroo	chimney
lorry	gnu
turkey	torpedo
commando	portfolio
kimono	trolley
tomato	wharf

wolf	city
studio	piano
soprano	jockey
igloo	flamingo
calf	potato

Revision exercises

Exercise 19
Fill the gaps in the following words:

deter _____ ate	exa _____ erate
rec __ g __ ise	suc ___ sful
para ____ el	vete _____ ary

Exercise 20
Tick the right and correct the wrong spellings below:

seperate	committee
miscellaneous	particuly
acomodate	changable
volcanos	ocasionally
contemperary	inoculate
recurrence	recieve
weird	posessions

Exercise 21
Fill the gap in each sentence below by choosing the correct word from the list:

maximum, maxima
parenthesis, parentheses
formula, formulae
phenomenon, phenomena
medium, media
stratum, strata

1 A great many strange _____ have been reported by our investigator at the haunted house.
2 People tend to refer loosely to 'the _____', meaning, in general, radio, television, and the popular press.
3 When archaeologists start a dig they first take very careful note of the various _____ of different materials that are revealed.
4 Doing chemistry at school does mean learning quite a lot of complicated _____ .
5 What is the _____ number of passengers the new bus can carry?
6 If written comments placed in _____ are lengthy there is a danger that the reader will lose the sense of the passage.

Exercise 22

Underline and correct the mistakes in the following passage:

My sisters eyes' widened as she surveyed my crumbling cieling. I waited untill she had recovered herself. 'Your prophesy is fullfilled', I said. 'It happenned last night'.

Alicia was visibly effected. She siezed my hand, 'Im coming to help with this' she said. 'Ive a comittee meeting this morning to discuss the accomodation for the VIP's who are arriving next week, but after that Im free. Why dont you do your clarinet practise in the bedroom this morning? Ill be back by lunchtime.'

With the prospect of a concert in two weeks time, I was glad to be relieved of the burden of clearing up alone. Alicias eficiency was as remarkable as her beauty, and I knew she excelled as a painter and decorater. Once we had cleared the room, and the ceilings plaster had been renewed, restoration would procede apace under her managment.

As I shook the dust from my music, before takeing it to the bedroom, I heard a kind of scrapeing noise that seemed to be comeing from above the exposed laths of the cieling. Fearful of a reccurence of the nights event, I made for the door, glanceing as I did so at the hole above.

It was the moment of crises. Even now I can hear the unmanly shreik that escaped me as I dived into the hall, slaming the door behind me. For my swift glance had percieved a horror almost beyond my minds belief: the slithering, sinuous, ploping descent from between the exposed laths of the ceiling, of a large, befanged, and apallingly evil-looking snake.

Exercise 23
Complete the unfinished words in the sentences below:

1 A fault at the transmitt_____ prevented our hearing the end of the programme.
2 The newsagent's shop at the corner sells station_____ and con-fection_____ as well as cigarettes, ice cream and mi_____el-lan_____ous items.
3 I never know whether faulty goods should be returned to the purvey_____ or the manufactur_____.
4 Is he the invent_____ of the strange propell_____ we saw in the workshop?
5 She is the proud possess_____ of a comput_____.

Exercise 24
Correct the mistakes in the following sentences:

1 Please give Mr Jone's his prescription.
2 Tell me about Theseus's heroic exploits.
3 Our tomatoes are ripening now and we're diging the main crop potatos.
4 He fixed his melancholy gaze on the cities chimnies and roofes.
5 That lorries cab is not like the cabs of the other lorries.
6 Its a glorious day at the Oval today.
7 What a nuisance it is when ones relations arrive unannounced.
8 I'm going to talk to the principle lecturer to ask his advise about the matter.

3 Punctuation

Punctuation marks help to make meanings clear. They indicate pauses and emphases and the ways in which words are grouped. Good punctuation is scarcely noticeable. When it is not good, understanding is made difficult or even impossible.

There are rules of punctuation but they do not govern minor points. This means that the small details of punctuation may vary from person to person. In particular, people differ over the use of the comma. The tendency nowadays is to punctuate as sparely as possible.

Whatever you feel about the details of punctuation, your aim should be to use it to make your meaning entirely clear and unambiguous.

Full stops and capital letters

Sentences begin with capital letters and end with full stops. The exceptions to this rule are sentences that are direct questions or exclamations. These end with their appropriate marks (? and !).

38

A sentence is a group of words that makes complete sense and that contains a finite verb, that is, a verb with a subject:

The crowd cheered.

In that sentence the finite verb is *cheered*; its subject is *the crowd.*

Exercise 1

Supply full stops to those groups of words below that are sentences:

1 I am unhappy
2 Buckingham Palace, the stately centre of the capital city
3 Crossing the open space, quietly and cautiously, and watching all the time for the reappearance of the gunman
4 The potter's strong hands, cupped loosely round the dark ball of clay, suddenly tensed
5 Germs can kill

Answers for Chapter 3 are on pp. 179–87.

Capital letters, as well as being used for the initial letters of sentences, are used for the initial letters of names of places, persons, months, days, and nationalities. They are used also for the titles of organisations (e.g. the British Academy), and for particular events and eras (e.g. the Glorious Revolution, the Stone Age). Capitals are not used for the seasons of the year or the points of the compass. A useful rule to remember is that capitals should be used for the particular and small letters for the general:

The Archbishop of York welcomed the visiting archbishops.

Exercise 2

Supply full stops, capital letters, and question and exclamation marks where necessary in the following:

1 we meet on the last wednesday of each month, except in july and august last month we visited the national gallery in london
2 the royal mile is the name of a famous street in edinburgh have you ever been there
3 we are planning an expedition to the swiss alps so that we can photograph the lovely alpine flowers
4 what a surprise whoever thought of this marvellous idea
5 she reads the bible regularly and knows a great deal about biblical characters
6 are they both members of the ambridge social club

Initial capitals are used for all the main words in the titles of books, plays, documents, and articles, e.g.

The Shorter Oxford English Dictionary
As You Like It
'The Art of the Renaissance'

Exercise 3

Rewrite the sentences below, correcting any errors of punctuation and supplying or deleting capital letters where necessary:

1 We shall have to book a flight from gatwick Airport do you mind having to fly.
2 He applied for a job with the British broadcasting corporation
3 do you know the painting called 'Virgin of the rocks' by Leonardo da vinci.
4 All the new peers will assemble in the House of lords today What a spectacle that will be.

At one time it was common practice to use stops with all initials and abbreviations. Thus we would see, and write, 'B.B.C.', 'T.V.', 'R.S.V.P.', 'Mr.', 'Dr.', and so on. But practice has changed, and it is now acceptable to omit stops from capital initials such as BBC, TV, UK.

The placing of stops after abbreviations is fully discussed in Chapter 6 (p. 118) but a widely accepted rule is that if the abbreviated form of a word ends with the same letter as the full form, including plurals, then it is not given a full stop, e.g.

Mr	*but*	Esq.
Dr		The Rev.
Mrs		p. (page)
vols (volumes)		no. (number)

The initials of forenames and Christian names are given stops.

Exercise 4
Supply or delete stops where necessary and correct all errors in the following:

1 Mr. W Smith lives in Blossom drive, next door to the Rev James Brown
2 Have you a copy of *An A.B.C. of English usage*.
3 P.C Smith of the Devon constabulary is to appear on TV
4 Miss. Jane Wilton has sent me a party invitation I see that it has an R.S.V.P. note on it.

The comma

The comma is the lightest of all the punctuation pauses, yet its placing can radically alter the sense and emphasis of words. It should be used with care and only when there is genuine work for it to do. The exercises in this section draw attention to misuses as well as to the proper uses of the comma, for we learn to use it effectively and well by becoming sensitive to its limitations and scope.

Exercise 5

Which of the sentences below are incorrectly punctuated? Say briefly what is wrong with each incorrect sentence:

1 She came, as she always did after matins on Sunday morning.
2 The vase, a fine Ming specimen, was sold by auction.
3 At last his hand found the lever, and with a last desperate effort, he raised the lid.
4 He wrote a short, rude, and extremely upsetting letter.

Let us look at three main uses of the comma.

● Commas to separate listed items:

As we dug over the allotment we came across an old tin tub, a flat iron, numerous bed springs, and the remains of an old gas cooker.

It could be argued that there is no need to place a comma before the 'and' in that sentence because the 'and' itself does the work of separating the last item from the others. This is really a matter of taste. My own preference is for placing a comma before the 'and' because I like the pause before the last item as well as before the earlier ones. With certain types of sentences it is essential to place a comma before the 'and' in order to avoid ambiguity. Consider the following example, in which a list of shops is given:

In London we visited Harrods, Selfridges, D. H. Evans, Liberty, and Marks and Spencer.

Without the comma before 'and Marks and Spencer' it would not be clear that 'Marks and Spencer' is one firm.

● Commas to separate descriptive words:

His tall, thin, stooping figure was often seen shuffling along the meaner, shabbier streets of the town.

But note that descriptive words are separated by commas

only when each word *acts independently on the word described*. Consider the difference in meaning between

We are using new, experimental methods

and

We are using new experimental methods.

● Commas to mark off a phrase, or phrases, within a sentence:

The new books, carefully packed in padded boxes, were delivered in the early morning.

Exercise 6
Add commas where needed in the sentences below:

1 Strange words obscure allusions references to abstract ideas here and there do not make a poem an important one.
2 Freud thought that art was a substitute for power honour riches and the love of women.
3 The Surrealists wanted to dive into the subconscious mind the mind below the conscious surface and dig up the images from there.
4 During the First World War three poets died who if they had survived would surely have altered the prevailing standards of poetry.
5 This anthology of critical essays will I hope be of interest to all students of poetry.

Long sentences, especially those that build up a detailed description, require a careful placing of commas:

Music too could work the same spell between them, dissolving the wall of this too solid world, softening Lytton's heart, unlearning his mind, and stirring, with trembling compression, his whole being until it seemed to float, weightless and unsubstantial, like the airs that crept so softly upon the harp-strings and filled the silence of the spheres with their legendary echoes.

Michael Holroyd, *Lytton Strachey*, p. 941

That sentence contains eight commas and could well, in the hands of some writers, have been given three more. The sentence might have begun: 'Music, too, could...', and a further comma might have been placed after the word 'being'. Again, this is not so much a matter of correctness or incorrectness as of taste and judgement concerning what best suits the sense, structure, and flow of the sentence.

Exercise 7

Place commas appropriately in the following sentence:

Though his rowdy spirits and Georgian athleticism were sometimes too excessive for Lytton's indoor tastes yet Garnett's robust good looks his unabashed conceit his unselfconscious manner his matter-of-fact imagination and vivid response to the physical and materialistic side of living coupled with a strain of modern sensibility were of a type to which Lytton felt himself inevitably drawn.

Holroyd, p. 697

The comma is often incorrectly used between two groups of words which are really independent sentences:

Francis Bacon was not a progressive thinker, he did not comprehend the full import of the new mathematical ideas of his time.

Either a full stop should be placed after 'thinker', or the two sentences should be joined by an 'and' to make one complex sentence.

A common failing is to use one comma where a pair of commas should be used:

The great house, though decayed and neglected looked magnificent under that dark and stormy sky.

A second comma should be placed after 'neglected'.

Exercise 8

1–5 below are examples of incorrect or insufficient uses of commas. Rewrite them, punctuating them correctly.

1 He wrote requesting an explanation, this letter was followed by a more peremptory demand.
2 The weather, hitherto soft and balmy has suddenly become cold wet and thoroughly wintry.
3 Used properly with regard for its various functions the comma is an excellent aid, and tool for the writer.
4 Disraeli was an author as well as a politician, he wrote several novels.
5 At last and just as we were feeling that all hope was gone, we saw a steady gleam of light on the high moor.

The semicolon and the colon

The semicolon (;) is an extremely useful punctuation mark. It marks a pause longer than a comma, but does not impose the finality of a full stop:

His conduct revealed no malevolence; it can only be described as neutral, or indifferent.

To use a comma after 'malevolence' would be straightforwardly wrong; and a full stop would produce a staccato effect:

His conduct revealed no malevolence. It can only be described as neutral, or indifferent.

The semicolon is particularly useful in that it can separate ideas and yet maintain connexions between them by keeping them within a single sentence:

Train yourself to be alert to all kinds of solecisms; read the papers with a critical eye; listen carefully to radio news bulletins; above all, take notice of all that is said by sports commentators on radio and television.

Exercise 9

Punctuate the following sentences, using commas and semi-colons:

1 The poem has its own existence apart from us it was there before us and will endure after us.
2 Modern man has not found substitutes for wheat barley oats and rice nor has he domesticated new animals as beasts of burden.
3 Technology sometimes produces ecological mishaps it also invents the means to deal with them.
4 He had nothing to do with the crime so we need not interrogate him nor need we trouble his wife with questions.

Exercise 10

Capitalise and punctuate the following passage:

oliver sat down slowly his hand held to his brow he was completely bewildered what was he to do now he could try to escape on the other hand to stay with these robbers in the hills might be a way of finding out what he wanted to know if he attempted to escape he would probably be shot in the back nothing could be achieved in that way he would remain

The colon (:) was once used a good deal as a kind of lesser full stop. It occurs throughout the Bible:

Let not mercy and truth forsake thee: bind them about thy neck; write them upon the table of thine heart:
So shalt thou find favour and good understanding in the sight of God and man.

Proverbs, iii, 3–4

The main use of the colon nowadays is to *introduce* matter that explains or elaborates something already mentioned. I have used it regularly in these chapters to introduce examples and exercises. The following sentence shows it at work as an introducer:

For William Gilbert the universe had no centre: every physical body was independent, and possessed a magnetic force which attracted other bodies to its own surface.

The colon may also be used to introduce a quotation:

Consider the line: 'Glory be to God for dappled things'.

Exercise 11
Place colons appropriately in the sentences below:

1 The taste of an adolescent writer is intense but narrow it is determined by personal needs.
2 There are two forms of impersonality that which is natural to the mere skilful craftsman, and that which is more and more achieved by the maturing artist.
3 To sum up education must be education for every aspect of life.
4 The Greek thinkers launched mankind into a new search the search for a system that integrated man with the world.
5 My life had changed radically I had a regular income, a room of my own, and an enchanting girlfriend.

You are unlikely to misuse the colon if you keep it solely for the work of *introducing*, a function succinctly described by Fowler (*Modern English Usage*, p. 589) as 'delivering the goods that have been invoiced in the preceding words'. But its older and less familiar function of providing a distinct, presaging pause should not be forgotten. Under the hand of a skilful writer, the colon can be used with subtle dramatic effect:

This was, no doubt, a settlement of prosperous businessmen; a reservation, like those created for indigenous inhabitants, or wild animal life, in some region invaded by alien elements: a kind of refuge for beings unfitted to battle with modern conditions, where they might live their own lives, undisturbed and unexploited by an aggressive outer world. In these confines the species might be saved from extinction. I felt miles away from everything, lying there in that bedroom: almost as if I were abroad.

Anthony Powell, *The Acceptance World*, p. 74

Exercise 12

Punctuate and capitalise the following passage using the full stop, the comma, the semicolon and the colon:

there was much to be done an acre of old garden to be revived outbuildings to be repaired cleaned and returned to use the whole house to be opened and aired restored and made warmly habitable they felt deeply happy at the prospect of years of honest exhausting toil lying before them mollie had secret plans for a mushroom bed vines melons and peppers william true to habit began to keep a written record of their days he bought a large stiff-bound book for the purpose and marked it in sections kitchen garden house outbuildings paddock stables and so on the great project dreamed-of for so long had at last begun

Quotation marks

The main use of quotation marks is to denote direct speech; that is, the *actual words* of a speaker:

When I asked him what he thought of classical music, he said, 'I never think about it at all'.

Note the following features of the punctuation of the above example:

● *Single* quotation marks ('') are used to enclose the speaker's words. It is now a widely accepted practice to

48

keep double quotation marks (" ") for quotations, names, or titles occurring *within* quotations:

He then remarked, very crossly, 'I suppose you'll now say, "Well you ought to think about it", or some such rubbish'.

- The final full stop is placed *outside* the closing quotation mark. This rule holds for any quotation that is part of a sentence that introduces or comments on it, even though the quotation itself may be a complete sentence. A quotation that is not part of a commenting or introductory sentence may have its stop placed *inside* the quotation marks.

- A comma is placed after the 'said' that precedes the quotation of direct speech. This is customary with verbs of saying that either introduce or follow quoted speech:

He remarked, 'It's a lovely day'.

And:

'It's a lovely day', he remarked, 'and one we shall always remember'.

Although this practice is fairly general it is one that is often debated and it should not be regarded as a firm rule. It could be argued that the commas on either side of 'he remarked' in my second example are fussy, and not essential to the meaning or tone of the sentence.

It is easy to make small mistakes when quoting direct speech:

My tutor said that I was 'one of her best students'.

The actual words of the tutor were presumably '. . . one of *my* best students'. The sentence therefore needs recasting, either to introduce the actual words correctly, or to present the tutor's remark as *indirect* speech; that is, without using quotation marks:

My tutor said to me, 'You are one of my best students'.

Or:

My tutor said that I was one of her best students.

Exercise 13

Punctuate the following, using quotation marks where necessary:

1 Smiling she answered Yes I shall be there tomorrow
2 The Chancellor of the Exchequer speaking on television said that nothing would be allowed to weaken his new anti-inflation measures
3 Do you know that poem by Ted Hughes that begins October is marigold
4 Boltzman said in a lecture entropy is a measure of physical probability

So far, I have outlined just a few generally acceptable practices for punctuating sentences containing quotations. It would be possible to give more information about the placing of commas and question marks, about the denotation of titles and quotations within quotations, and so on; but practice concerning these details varies considerably and general rules cannot be formulated. For instance, one controversial difficulty arises when a quoted question occurs at the end of a sentence which is itself a question. Strictly speaking, two question marks are then required:

How does one give a short answer to the person who asks, 'How does a silicon chip work?'?

However, in that kind of sentence, no confusion or ambiguity results from allowing one question mark to do the work of two, and so we might as well write:

How does one give a short answer to the person who asks, 'How does a silicon chip work'?

When you have to deal with a punctuation difficulty of that sort, try to work out a procedure that makes your meaning completely clear and that avoids unnecessary or fussy punctuation. Be consistent in your use of whatever procedure you adopt.

Exercise 14

Punctuate the following:

1 His actual words were Tennyson's technical competence is never less than masterly
2 Tell me at once he said what you mean by that
3 Can you remember that speech in *Hamlet* that begins To be or not to be
4 It continues with the words that is the question doesn't it

There are three further and fairly straightforward uses of quotation marks. The first is to denote a word or phrase that is being singled out for comment, explanation, or discussion:

The word 'situation' is greatly over-used these days.

The second is to show that a word or phrase is not being used in its standard sense, or that an invented or slang word is being used. When used in this way quotation marks are often called 'scare-quotes'. Sometimes a word is given scare-quotes to show that it is being used ironically:

We shall have to find out what the computer 'thinks' about these statistics.

The third additional use is to enclose the names or titles of poems, pieces of music, articles, papers, paintings, essays and broadcasts:

Do you know Mendelssohn's 'Wedding March'?

Titles of books, plays, newspapers, magazines, journals and pamphlets should not be placed within quotation marks. In print they appear in italics, and in writing or typescript they should be underlined. (This topic is dealt with in greater detail in Chapter 6.)

Exercise 15

Punctuate and capitalise the following:

1 have you ever watched the TV programme called coronation street
2 When I said that I thought the mona lisa was a very great painting he replied it is all a matter of taste
3 I shall have to look up the word echelon in my dictionary
4 We have designed an electronic mouse and are about to test it to see if it can escape from a maze
5 Mr Gladstone used to say the photograph cannot lie

Dashes, brackets, and hyphens

Dashes or brackets may be used to enclose a remark or statement that is inserted into a sentence as an 'aside' or as an extra comment or explanation. This kind of 'aside' is called a *parenthesis*. The test of a parenthesis, it is sometimes said, is whether the other words make sense without it:

If the orbits of the planets were exact circles – as they were once thought to be – then each planet would exhibit a constant tendency to the centre.

And:

There are many further problems to be considered (moral, political, social, technical) before we can attempt to make any judgements and decisions.

A less pronounced, but much-used kind of parenthesis is one that is placed between commas:

It was, as you have already recognised, an extremely difficult experiment to carry out accurately.

I do not recommend more than a very occasional use of dashes to mark parentheses in essays and academic writing. Their visual impression on the reader is usually one of haste, or of a last-minute attempt to incorporate near-forgotten thoughts into a passage. However, an occasional, apt use of them can give prominence to a point that might otherwise be overlooked:

Many ecologists describe themselves as conservationists, and their aim – a different aim from that of the preservationists – is to conserve natural resources for future use.

Brackets are probably used more often than dashes for parentheses in academic writing. But they, too, should be used sparingly for their over-use has the effect of breaking up writing so that the reader has the feeling that the main flow of ideas never really gets going. The difference between bracketed parentheses and those within dashes is not easy to pinpoint: brackets tend to separate their contents sharply from the surrounding matter, giving them the status of an optional addition to the main sentence; dashes tend to maintain what they enclose at the same level as the rest of the sentence. Very often a pair of commas will do all that is required.

Exercise 16
Indicate the parentheses in the sentences below with the marks you think most suitable ((...), –...–, or ,...,).

1 St Paul has said that the woman I cite the authorised version of the Bible is not to usurp authority over the man.
2 There is strong evidence that an exploding star a supernova provided the material of the Earth.
3 The third question which is the most searching one by far will take a little longer to answer.
4 Nearly all flowering plants which means nearly all the higher plants are dependent on birds and insects for pollination.
5 Oliver Cromwell and regicide ensured that England would be ruled by parliaments, and not by kings.

A single dash is often used to denote a pause that precedes a summary or amplification; used thus, it does work similar to that of the 'introductory' colon, though in a less formal way:

Stoics believed that the universe was organised to serve the interests of its only rational inhabitants – men and gods.

There are more dubious uses of the dash. It is not an all-purpose punctuation mark that can save the trouble of writing a properly constructed sentence. The following illustrates a sloppy and unnecessary use of dashes:

Foreign travel – provided that one likes it – is always stimulating, and usually good value for money – even the very small European hotels usually have a pleasant atmosphere and interesting food – not to mention an abundance of local colour.

I am being hard on dashes because they so often mar rather than improve academic writing. But under the hand of a gifted, imaginative writer, the dash can be a subtle and versatile tool. Look at a copy of Laurence Sterne's *Tristram Shandy* and see how he uses the dash, and how essential it is to his particular style.

In academic writing brackets are used a great deal more than parentheses. They can enclose references, reminders, page and chapter numbers, and short explanations or pieces of information that the writer wishes to make available without disrupting the flow of a passage. Here are three examples:

This will be dealt with more fully later on (see Chapter V).

He writes first of freedom *from* various restraints (pp. 10–12), and then of freedom to act in particular matters of his own choosing (pp. 13–18).

Let us try to pick out and discuss critically two or three examples of persiflage (ironic talk, the seriousness of which is difficult to judge).

Exercise 17

Which of the sentences below use dashes in an acceptable way? Rewrite any sentences that do not:

1 It's her shorthand – not her typing – that must be improved.
2 They were impressed by a number of items – the old Welsh dresser for one – and thought the whole house had been most cleverly converted and decorated – even noting the careful restoration of the old door locks.
3 We have inherited a great tradition – one that is as old as our parliamentary system.
4 He had said before – and would no doubt say again – that a free market economy could not provide a way out of our economic difficulties.

Hyphens are used to indicate that two or more words are to be read together as a single word. Many pairs of words which were once hyphenated have been combined to make single words. Thus, 'boatman' was once 'boat-man', 'handkerchief' was once 'hand-kerchief', and so on. Some pairings are still indeterminate; we see 'goodnight' and 'good-night', 'handshake' and 'hand-shake', 'scrapbook' and 'scrap-book'. Good judgement, observation, and a dictionary are needed to guide our use of hyphens.

Hyphens should always be placed between words which, if combined, would produce awkward juxtapositions of letters:

looking-glass	*not*	lookingglass
public-house	*not*	publichouse
re-enter	*not*	reenter

Exercise 18

Insert hyphens where necessary in the following sentences:

1 Shall you be at the end of term prize giving?
2 In the back street, they found a little frequented restaurant.
3 He is an authority on the nineteenth century English novelists.
4 She has a happy go lucky disposition.
5 I'd love to own a fried fish shop.

Hyphens are useful aids to understanding. They should be used only when they are necessary for making meanings clear. It is best to avoid the practice of separating a pair of hyphenated words, leaving a hyphen in mid-air, as in:

I am willing to do full- or part-time work.

It is better to write:

I am willing to do full-time or part-time work.

Exercise 19

Insert or delete hyphens appropriately in the sentences below:

1 This piece of research is a government financed project.
2 The murder took place in a first class carriage.
3 My publishing firm has just brought out a paper-back about the battle-fields of the First World War.
4 This book jacket is so badly torn that I think we shall have to recover it.
5 This is a handsome coat of arms belonging to a well known family.
6 As a disc jockey he is well known.

Revision exercises

Exercise 20
Supply capital letters and full stops to the following:

the german sociologist max weber died at about five o'clock on the afternoon of june 14, 1920 the day had been wet and when weber's student karl loewenstein visited the weber home on the seestrasse in munich he found the sick man alone for a few minutes loewenstein stayed by the bed, watching the last struggles of his teacher then he left weber's wife marianne was elsewhere in the house, resting shortly after loewenstein's departure weber died, unattended and solitary

Donald G. MacRae, *Weber*, p. 11

Exercise 21
Supply capital letters, full stops, inverted commas, and question and exclamation marks where needed to the following:

1 have you a copy of the hymn jerusalem
2 What is mind what is matter how does one influence the other
3 During the first world war he was awarded a VC
4 Mr and Mrs T Jones walked slowly away from the house in Victoria street

Exercise 22
Supply commas to the following sentences:

1 Anthropologists used to distinguish between Culture conceived of as exclusively human and Nature which was common to all animals.
2 An experienced anthropologist may after spending a few days with a primitive society be able to see exactly how the society's social system works.
3 For the next expedition he bought a small pocket-knife a billy-

can some bandages and plasters and three pairs of wool and
nylon socks.
4 This process is new experimental slightly risky and very
expensive.

Exercise 23
Capitalise and punctuate the following:

already by the late 1880s it was obvious that the family was in
decline now as the victorian age tottered towards its exhausted
conclusion and the first grumblings of serious reaction made themselves heard they looked about and for the first time found themselves out of touch with the rising mood but within the arid and
forbidding precincts of lancaster gate everything remained as
before unchanged and unchangeable being invited there for the first
time was an odd sometimes even alarming experience like stepping
into another age perhaps another world

Michael Holroyd, *Lytton Strachey*, p. 45

Exercise 24
Place colons and semicolons where needed in the following
sentences:

1 Classical physics introduced two substances matter and energy.
2 The theory of relativity disposes of the difficulties of the field
   theory it formulates wider mechanical laws it replaces two conservation laws with one it changes our concept of time.
3 Do not be afraid of the semi-colon it can be most useful.
4 His purpose was twofold he would survey the job prospects, and
   also explore further a part of the country he had always wanted
   to revisit.

Exercise 25

Punctuate and supply quotation marks where necessary to the following:

1 He said that all being well he would visit her next week
2 What exactly does the phrase turned on mean
3 He stated his main theme in the following words this party will not be re-elected until it becomes a united party
4 The doctor said to him you must rest for at least a week
5 Did he say when is she going or where is she going
6 Helen asked what did he mean when he whispered tread softly to you

Exercise 26

Insert suitable marks of parenthesis where necessary in the following sentences:

1 We should be prepared to prohibit a pollutant an insecticide, for instance until its long-term effects are known.
2 Man's great memorials his science, his philosophy, his technology, his architecture, his countryside are all founded on his attempt to subdue nature.
3 The three attempts at reconciliation already described in detail on pp. 82–98 did eventually generate some useful discussion.

Exercise 27

Correct any faults of hyphenation in the following:

1 To-morrow we shall be meeting the new head-master.
2 Every cat owning householder should have a cat door.
3 My own view is that the Abominable Snowman is nonexistent.
4 We shall not succeed without your cooperation.
5 The programme contains both high- and low-brow music.

4 Grammar

Grammar becomes important when bad grammar makes writing imprecise or ambiguous. Without a grammar, that is, without rules to govern the arrangement of words and the making of their plurals, tenses, and so on, meanings could not be made clear by writers or understood by readers. There are no fixed, unchangeable rules of correct grammar, but there is a large and solid body of accepted practice which, if used widely and consistently, enables us to make our meanings exact.

In this chapter we shall look at some grammatical failings that affect clarity and meaning, and also at some controversial points of grammar.

Arranging the words

Even when the words of a sentence are so badly arranged that they do not say what their writer or speaker meant them to say, we are often able to guess the intended meaning. We all know what was meant by the eager shop assistant who, when he had fitted his customer with a sober-looking grey suit, stepped back admiringly and said, 'You can't fail to go wrong in that, sir'. Often a change in the order of the words, or some small alteration, deletion, or addition will put matters right. However, it isn't always possible to see what a careless writer is trying to say. For instance, there are two possible meanings of the following sentence:

Miss Green told Miss White that she was to receive a pay increase.

Ambiguities of that kind are not easily noticed when you are actually writing. Be on the lookout for them when you read through your completed work.

Exercise 1

Rewrite the sentences below to make their meanings clear:

1 The present administration led by an experienced prime minister, now a year old, is pursuing a policy of free trade.
2 Some shots were fired at the terrorists' car, and after travelling several miles at high speed, a bullet shattered the rear window.
3 He announced that there would be a discussion on motorbikes in the church vestry.

Answers for Chapter 4 are on pp. 188–94.

A common cause of unclear meaning is a phrase that is not related to the rest of the sentence in which it occurs. This sort of phrase is often called *a dangling modifier*. A modifier is a word or phrase that makes more exact the meaning of some other words, and if the modifier does not relate correctly to the words it is meant to modify then it is as if it is left dangling, or unattached, and we are not quite sure where it belongs:

Being thoroughly mildewy, he threw the cheese away.

There the modifier is 'being thoroughly mildewy' and it is meant to modify 'the cheese'. But the grammatical meaning of the sentence is that *he* was *thoroughly mildewy* and *threw the cheese away*. The modifying phrase was not attached to its proper subject; it was left dangling, and had to seize a foothold in the only possible place – on the word 'he'.

One way of avoiding that kind of error is to place the modifier as close as possible to the word or words that it modifies:

Being thoroughly mildewy, the cheese was thrown away.

That construction, although correct and acceptable, leaves out any mention of 'he'. It also uses the passive voice in a way that produces a rather stilted style. We can change all that, if we wish, by altering the structure of the sentence:

As the cheese was thoroughly mildewy, he threw it away.

Or:

He threw away the cheese because it was thoroughly mildewy.

Exercise 2

Rewrite the following sentences to make their meanings clear:

1 When only a small child, my father took me to the Science Museum.
2 Driving across India, our money ran out.
3 After staying with his patients all morning, in spite of other engagements, the doctor went on his usual round of the wards.
4 An appeal for the restoration of the old Guildhall by the secretary of the Community Association has just been launched.
5 He ran a seminar yesterday on intensive pig-rearing in the senior common room.

Some common failings

Quite often we read or hear a sentence of the following sort:

Due to the damp, the manuscripts had disintegrated.

That sentence is grammatically incorrect, and it is important to understand why. *Due to* means *caused by*. *Due* is an adjective* and an adjective is a word that describes a noun; but in the example above the phrase 'due to the damp' tries to relate itself to the verb 'disintegrated'. If we relate it, as it grammatically should be related, to the noun 'manuscripts', we would have to take it that the manuscripts were due to the damp. But this is not the intended meaning. To put things right we must change the verb *disintegrated* into a noun, so that 'due to the damp' describes what it is meant to describe:

The *disintegration* of the manuscripts was *due to the damp*.

Remember to use *due to* only when it can be related to a noun. If in doubt, use *owing to* or *because of* instead.

Exercise 3

Tick the sentences below that use *due to* correctly and rewrite those that are grammatically faulty, using *owing to* or *because of* if necessary:

1 The magpie, due to its spectacular black and white plumage, is easily detected in the countryside.
2 Due to the heavy floods, he was unable to attend the conference.
3 Her extreme lethargy was due to the heat.
4 Prices have increased due to the heavy demand.
5 Increased prices are due to the heavy demand.
6 His inability to deal with the cabinet crisis was due to the severe mental stress imposed on him during those terrible weeks.

Due to usually introduces an explanation, and it is sometimes combined with awkward or incorrect uses of other terms that introduce explanations. Thus we may see a phrase of the following kind:

---

* Except in compass directions: in 'due East', *due* is an adverb and means 'exactly'.

The reason for her failure is due to . . .

The phrase says too much. All that is needed is either

The reason for her failure is . . .

or

Her failure is due to . . .

or simply

She failed because . . .

When and *where* are sometimes used awkwardly in introducing explanations:

Osmosis is when . . .
The reason for photosynthesis is when . . .
Hadrian's Wall is where . . .

Again, too many words are being used. It is clearer and simpler to write:

Osmosis is . . .
Photosynthesis is . . .
Hadrian's Wall is . . .

Exercise 4
Write improved versions of the following:

1 The reason for the failure of the tests was due to a transcription error in the statistical data we used.
2 Due to a power failure, he caused the emergency generator to be switched on.
3 The reason for the breakdown in law and order was because of the bad handling of a quite minor incident.
4 The Bermuda Triangle is where there is an area of sea that is mysteriously dangerous.
5 The reason for blue litmus paper turning pink is when it is in contact with an acid.

The following sentences are incorrect:

We must plan our household economy so as to have less expenses.
He was advised to eat less eggs in order to cut down his cholesterol intake.

Both sentences should use *fewer* instead of *less*. *Fewer* applies to number, and is used with a plural noun. *Less* applies to quantity and degree, and is generally used with a singular noun. Thus:

Less trouble, less pleasure, less milk.
Fewer problems, fewer nails, fewer children.

Exercise 5

Supply the correct word (*less* or *fewer*) in the gap in each of the following sentences:

1 This disappointing exhibition contains a mere handful of auto-graphed copies and even _____ first editions.
2 If the wearing of car safety-belts were made compulsory, would there be _____ road deaths?
3 We require a policy that guarantees _____ unemployment.
4 By now you should be making _____ grammatical mistakes.
5 She has done _____ essay-writing than all the other students in her year.
6 I shall oppose any scheme that offers _____ opportunities to our engineering graduates.

Lay and *lie* are frequently misused. It is helpful to remember that the verb *to lay* always requires mention of something that is laid: it is a transitive verb, that is, a verb that has an object. Thus, a hen lays *eggs*, a DIY expert lays a *carpet*, a gamekeeper lays a *trap*, and so on.

Lie is not a transitive verb. In 'he is lying down', *down* is not something that he is laying, as a hen lays eggs; it simply describes his lying. Confusions can arise over the past tense of *to lie*, for the past tense of 'he is lying down' is 'he lay down'. *Laid*, as a past tense, belongs only with the transitive verb *to lay*: 'The hen *laid* six brown eggs last week'.

Exercise 6
All the sentences below use *to lay* and *to lie* incorrectly. Correct them:

1 We laid out on a sunny hillside all day.
2 She was lying out the cards in rows on the table.
3 If you are feeling faint you should lay on the bed.
4 We left the body where it laid.
5 They are lying down new regulations for entry to the chess congress.
6 The terrified dog laid absolutely still and silent.

Prepositions

The English language abounds in prepositions. *In, on, at, over, along, with, under, to, from, of, by, upon, after, down, across* are examples of prepositions. A preposition is used with a noun, or with a word that is the equivalent of a noun, to relate it to a verb, or to an adjective, or to another noun:

The Queen walked steadily *across* the courtyard, *under* the stone arch, and then *up* the narrow steps *to* the terrible, hard scaffold.

Because there are a great many prepositions, and because they occur so often and in so many ways, clumsy or careless use of them can affect the clarity of writing. There are no absolutely rigid rules that govern the use of prepositions; once again, it is established practice that determines what is sensible and clear. You should therefore take my judgements as no more than guides to accepted practice, and not as rules requiring unquestioning obedience. What is important is to be aware of possible uses and to think carefully about which preposition best suits your meaning.

Exercise 7

Cross out the unsuitable prepositions in the sentences below:

1 His work cannot be judged solely on/by/through the short stories.
2 The Jarrow marchers walked to London to protest at/over/against unemployment.
3 Picasso's earlier paintings are markedly different from/to/than his later ones.
4 He is conducting a survey into/about/of the sales techniques of two major car firms.
5 She was so engrossed that she was oblivious of/to/with the time.
6 The new regime was remarkably tolerant of/to/about certain corrupt practices in the administrative services.
7 He was a poor substitute to/for/by his predecessor.
8 We think the charity should continue to work independently from/of/to any political bodies.

Exercise 8

Supply prepositions to the following:

1 He suffers _____ arthritis.
2 Is there no alternative _____ redundancy?
3 You will have to replace it _____ a new one.
4 I shall aim _____ doing six hours work every day.
5 The stainless steel dish is inferior _____ the silver one.
6 They agreed _____ the proposal.
7 I agreed _____ John.
8 She refuses to conform _____ the rules.

Using too many prepositions and using prepositions unnecessarily are common failings. In the sentence

The power point must be fixed *outside of* the bathroom

the preposition *of* does no work at all; *outside* is sufficient by itself:

The power point must be fixed outside the bathroom.

Exercise 9
Delete any superfluous prepositions from the following sentences:

1 If the tank is not completely emptied out, this method will not give accurate results.
2 The two men are preparing to climb up the mountain.
3 The new instructions were given just as they were entering into the space capsule.
4 We shall have to recall back two of the candidates.
5 These sunflowers grow to heights of from seven to twelve feet.
6 There are fears that the violence will recur again.
7 We should divide up the routine jobs between us.

'Never end a sentence with a preposition' is a well-known piece of grammatical advice that common sense, idiom, and usage tend to ignore. It is the 'never' that is unacceptable; for although some sentences have a better shape and rhythm when the advice is followed, others are grotesquely contorted by the avoidance of a final preposition. Thus:

They will cut *off* the gas

is probably a little better than

They will cut the gas *off*.

But the following is intolerable:

This is something *up with* which I will not put.

Instead we must have:

This is something I will not put *up with*.

And there seem to be no good reasons of either sense or sound for avoiding the final prepositions in the following:

Is the gas cut off?
What is the hammer for?
Collect up everything you can lay your hands on.

In the end we can only try to be alert to what makes for ease and lucidity in the use of prepositions, and then make our own judgements if difficulties occur.

Exercise 10
Tick the sentences below that you think are satisfactory, and write improved versions of any awkward ones:

1 It was the most taxing enterprise in which he had ever engaged.
2 You have to try to knock all the ninepins at the end of the gangway down.
3 What use will you put it to?
4 This is the place to put used envelopes in.
5 It is a difficult matter to sort out.
6 Remember to pick the ones that have fallen behind the desk up.
7 Let us see to what it amounts.

Some debatable points

'Never split an infinitive' was once an inflexible rule of grammar. Examples of infinitive forms of verbs are *to run*, *to travel*, *to understand*, *to regain*, *to swim*. In its infinitive form a verb is not limited to a particular subject such as *he*, *she*, *they*, and so on: it applies 'infinitely'. Infinitives are split by putting an adverb between the *to* and the verb:

To swiftly run ...
To arduously travel ...
To properly understand ...
To rapidly regain ...
To gracefully swim ...

The 'never split' rule is no longer inflexible. It is generally felt that wholesale and indiscriminate splitting of infinitives is undesirable, but that there may be times when clarity and sense require a split. Thus:

I wish to recompense you fully

is *preferred* to

I wish to fully recompense you

although the latter is no longer held to be 'bad grammar'. But a sentence of the following type should certainly be avoided:

Our purpose is *to* analytically, even at the expense of nullifying the aesthetic pleasure generated by the piece, *explore* the linguistic structure of every phrase of this impressive poem.

An unintentional change of meaning sometimes results from the attempt to avoid a split infinitive. Thus:

The soufflé failed to completely rise

should not be changed in order to avoid the split *to*

The soufflé completely failed to rise (wrong meaning)

nor to

The soufflé failed completely to rise (wrong meaning, *and* awkward style)

but to

The soufflé failed to rise completely.

Exercise 11

Rewrite the sentence below so as *not* to split the infinitives:

1 The work had begun to seriously affect his health.

2 The time has come to once again sweep up the dead leaves and light the autumn bonfire.
3 The architect has asked us to slightly enlarge the archway.
4 I urge you to humbly and generously acknowledge that your political opponents were right on this occasion.

The treatment of collective words, that is words that denote groups or collections of people or things, is controversial. Examples of collective words are: *congregation, herd, government, council, parliament, board, federation, the public, association, authority.* The question is, do we say:

The government has decided ...

or

The government have decided ... ?

The answer is that we may do as we choose. It is good practice to let the sense of a sentence help your choice. If the sentence inclines you to think of a group as a unified whole, then treat the collective word as a singular:

The committee *has* decided to act immediately.

If the sentence refers in some way to the individual activities of the members of the group, treating it as a singular may produce a slightly ludicrous effect:

The committee *has* left for *its* summer holidays.

Treat it therefore as a plural:

The committee *have* left for *their* summer holidays.

Inconsistent treatment of collective nouns is not acceptable:

The committee *has* left for *their* summer holidays.
The cabinet *have* met to discuss *its* future constitution.

Exercise 12

Correct or improve the treatment of the collective words in the following sentences:

1 The herd dispersed, kicking its heels and bellowing.
2 What does the public think about this outrage?
3 The Association are concerned with the building standards set by its members.
4 All the audience rose to its feet.

The use of *one* as a pronoun used to be encouraged on the grounds that it gave academic writing an impersonal and objective tone. But the trouble with *one*, as I shall now show, is that once one starts using it, one finds it sprouting up all over one's work. *One* must be used sparingly, and when it is used the use must be consistent. It will not do to write:

One tries to do your best.

The correct form is

One tries to do one's best.

In that sentence, *one's* is the possessive of *one*.

Exercise 13

Correct the sentences below to make the use of *one* consistent. Then rewrite each sentence avoiding any use of *one*:

1 As one reads the narrative of events, one realises that a large body of evidence is being presented for your consideration.
2 If you study during the same hours each day, one can acquire good work habits and improve your ability to concentrate.
3 When one applies for a job, you should expect to have one's credentials closely examined.

Common failings again

A verb must always agree with its subject; that is, a singular noun must have a singular verb, and a plural noun, or double or multiple subject, must have a plural verb. Mistakes are easily made when writing sentences in the following form:

The quality and colour of a fresco depends on careful preparation of the plaster wall.

In that sentence the verb 'depends' should be *depend*, as the subject is a double one: 'the quality and colour'. The writer was misled by the singular noun 'fresco' to use a singular verb.

Exercise 14

Correct any errors of agreement in the sentences below:

1 The imagery, diction, and syntax of each writer was examined.
2 From this study has come several new technical advances.
3 The skilled use of the new machines require careful training.
4 Evaluation of both teaching and research resources are necessary.
5 The dexterity of his movements are amazing.

There is often confusion over the use of *who* and *whom*. *Who* is used for the subject of a verb. Thus:

Who is to give this year's Reith Lectures?

And:

A London man *who is* a physicist is to give the Reith Lectures this year.

Whom is used for the object of a verb. Thus:

Whom are you *inviting* to judge the entries in the poetry competition? (You are inviting whom)

And:

He is a former colleague *whom* I've not *seen* for years. (I've not seen whom)

Whom is used with prepositions: to whom, from whom, with whom, by whom, for whom, etc. Thus:

For whom are the books intended?
These are the students *with whom* you will be working.
Whom was this written *by*?

Exercise 15

Fill the gaps in the following sentences:

1 He _____ hesitates is lost.
2 Praise God from _____ all blessings flow.
3 William Oughtred was the man _____ invented the equals sign.
4 He is someone for _____ I feel great sympathy.
5 _____ was the 'Old Hundredth' composed by?
6 I have no idea _____ he is.

Conjunctions are, on the whole, small words (*and*, *but*, *yet*, *nor*, *as*, *so*, *since*, *for*, *while*, etc.), but they can bring about large changes of meaning and should be used carefully. Conjunctions join phrases or words together, thereby allowing thought and language to move smoothly. They can also introduce shifts of emphasis and contrasting ideas:

The second movement has melodic charm *and* some pleasingly complex rhythms, *but* this young composer lacks the ability to sustain interest during a long movement.

Both *as* and *since* have several meanings, and you should always be alert to the risk of using them ambiguously. Consider the different meanings of the following uses:

Since you have come, you may as well join in. (since = as)
Life has been much pleasanter since you came. (since = ever since)
This change has taken place since you arrived. (since = between your arrival and now)
Since you have come, we will open another bottle. (since = because)
We can start the meeting, as the secretary has now arrived. (as = because)
The band will play as she mounts the steps to the hall. (as = while)
As you arrived, the fire alarm was sounded. (ambiguous: as = just as *or* because)
We could see she was not exhausted as she arrived first at the winning post. (ambiguous: as = at the moment *or* because)

Exercise 16
Cross out the incorrect conjunction in each of the sentences below:

1 Some of the melons were too hard, some were too soft, and/yet some were just right.
2 The theory, if/though not very convincing, is worth consideration.
3 While/although the children were very quiet, they did not seem to be afraid.
4 Neither the candidates or/nor the voters seem to be taking this election seriously.

Not so long ago it was held to be bad style to begin sentences with *And* or *But*. This is no longer the case. Sir Ernest Gowers points out that to use *And* to begin a paragraph is slightly affected. *But*, he says, may be used freely to begin either a sentence or a paragraph (*The Complete Plain Words*, p. 168).

Revision exercises

Exercise 17
Rewrite the following sentences to make their meanings clear:

1 A comfortable chair is wanted for an old-age pensioner with an adjustable back.
2 Perched on the high slab of rock, the rain was soaking him to the skin.
3 A letter of protest was sent to the men in triplicate.
4 The stolen coins were found by a policeman in a plastic bag.
5 She gave a lecture on the illegal distribution of cocaine and heroin to the Women's Institute.

Exercise 18
Supply or delete prepositions where necessary in the sentences below:

1 They shared out the spoils between them.
2 We were not told where we were being taken to.
3 The prince was always accompanied _____ a bodyguard.
4 The statue is opposite to the park gates.
5 When the gas escaped, the workmen were overcome _____ fumes.
6 That is not a good way for an essay to end up.

Exercise 19
Correct the sentences below, rewriting them if necessary:

1 Due to a fault at the transmitter, they were unable to relay the broadcast.
2 The reason for searching every room is because some dangerous drugs have disappeared.
3 We are not vegetarian, but we are trying to eat less meat meals.
4 The poetry course offers some seminars but less lectures than the novel course.

5 He laid injured in the ditch all night.
6 We shall lie down several bottles of this fine red wine.

Exercise 20

Rewrite the sentences below so as not to split the infinitives in them:

1 Anxiety and fear had begun to slowly and insidiously warp his powers of judgement.
2 You will have to gradually build up your stamina by swimming a little further each day.
3 Will it be possible to substantially and immediately increase the quality of this service?
4 He began to carefully explain the details of the technique.

Exercise 21

Fill the gaps in the sentences below in ways that are appropriate to the collective nouns:

1 The service was over, and the congregation _____ on _____ way home.
2 The board will let us know _____ decision tomorrow.
3 The scattered flock of sheep _____ bleating plaintively.
4 A small committee _____ elected to choose the books for the American Studies section of the library.
5 The family _____ unable to agree on a meeting place for the reunion.

Exercise 22

Cross out the incorrect words in the sentences below:

1 Whom/who shall I give the money to?
2 You should be able to tell from its style who/whom wrote that poem.

3 Those are the people whom/who I met on the archaeological dig.
4 In Venice he met a girl whom/who he fell in love with immediately.
5 She is someone who/whom we trust absolutely.

part two
Techniques

5 Style and diction

Some common failings   Diction: misused words
Ornate writing   Jargon   Vocabulary
Revision exercises

There is not one 'good style' that can serve the purposes of all kinds of writing: the style of a piece of imaginative prose, for instance, is very different from that of a scientific report or a history text book. A full discussion of the complex subject of style is far beyond the scope of this book. We shall therefore concentrate on clarity and directness of expression, and on identifying and correcting practices that usually produce bad style in academic writing. Good academic writing is clear, interesting, and well organised. Its style is appropriate to its purpose.

Good diction is important for good style. Insensitivity to the exact meanings of words generates confused writing and reading and a limited vocabulary means a limitation on your own thoughts. Many people are not absolutely clear about the meaning of the word 'diction'. If you are unsure, look it up in your dictionary before you go on to the exercises.

Some common failings

A clear style of writing is best achieved by becoming aware of and avoiding the bad habits and common errors that produce poor style. Poor writing is usually confused, over-elaborate, and difficult to understand. It often results from carelessness over the meanings of words.

In this section we shall look at some of the failings that characterise poor writing, and at ways of avoiding or correcting them.

Exercise 1
All the sentences below are examples of poor writing. For each sentence, underline the word or phrase that you think makes it poor, and try to say very briefly *why* it makes it poor. Write improved versions of the sentences if you can:

1 In the quarrel that followed the party, his wife was struck by him.
2 We were all shocked to hear of the chairman's very fatal final illness.
3 In this day and age, whilst industry is grinding to a halt, one can feel the wind of change heralding the arrival of a new climate of opinion.
4 In my view the remuneration received by the subordinate officials of this organisation exceeds by a very considerable proportion what is generally placed on offer by other comparable firms.
5 Their political opponents had proffered the olive branch, but nothing concrete had come out of it.
6 These economically attractive best quality refined chemicals will be on the market in three months' time.
7 The noise of the machinery rose to a steady crescendo.

Answers for Chapter 5 are on pp. 194–204.

Writing is often imprecise and ineffective because of the use of clichés. A cliché is a stereotyped phrase, once vividly effective but now worn out with careless over-use. There are countless well-established clichés such as *acid test*, *bitter end*, *conspicuous by his absence*, *sneaking suspicion*, *without a shadow of doubt*, *this day and age*, *at this moment in time*, *method in his madness*, *wearing a different hat*, *burning issue*, *wealth of information*, and so on. Writing that is full of clichés makes little impact on a reader. It seems to express stale, second-hand ideas, and it gives the impression that the writer has not bothered to make his or her own thoughts precise.

Exercise 2

Underline the clichés in the sentences below and rewrite the sentences as simply and clearly as possible:

1 We shall leave no stone unturned in our efforts to lend a helping hand.
2 It is of supreme and paramount importance to our education programme that classes should be kept at minimum levels.
3 In the senior common-room speculation was rife, but she remained as cool as a cucumber and took the situation in her stride.
4 Before we find ourselves at the tender mercies of those who are against us, let us explore every avenue to find a solution to the problem.

Hackneyed words and phrases are very similar to clichés, for the hackneyed expression is one that is trite or commonplace. In Fowler's *Modern English Usage* we read, 'There are thousands for whom the only sound sleep is the *sleep of the just*, the light at dusk must always be *dim*, *religious*; all beliefs are *cherished*, all confidence is *implicit*, all ignorance *blissful*, all isolation *splendid*, all uncertainty *glorious*, all voids *aching*'. Fowler warns that when such phrases come into a writer's mind he should take warning, 'because what he is writing is bad stuff, or it would not need such help' (pp. 234, 235).

Exercise 3

Underline the hackneyed phrases in the sentences below and rewrite the sentences:

1 It was extremely difficult to understand his essay because the commas in it were so few and far between.
2 Mary Queen of Scots spent many months in splendid isolation before Lord Shrewsbury, on 7 February 1587, arrived to read her death-warrant to her.
3 In *Hamlet Prince of Denmark*, Horatio remains loyal to the prince through thick and thin.
4 We shall not be able to go ahead with the scheme until we have the approval of the powers that be.
5 Mozart had the ability to write beautiful music even at a very tender age.

One of the commonest failings in poor writing is over-use of the passive voice. In exercise 1, the first example of poor writing showed an unnecessary use of the passive: '... his wife *was struck* by him'. Over-use of the passive usually creeps in when people try to write impersonal, objective descriptions of events or proceedings. We see sentences such as:

The new syllabus *has now been approved* by the Academic Committee.

A suggestion *was made* by Dr Jones that more time be made available for all tutorials.

Putting such sentences into the active voice makes them briefer, more direct, and more vigorous:

The Academic Committee has now approved the new syllabus.

Dr Jones suggested that all tutorials should last longer.

The passive voice has its proper uses. It can change the pace of a piece of writing, and emphasise what is important. For example:

He was injured in a car crash.

She was given numerous bouquets and presents.

The new chairman *has been appointed*.

A lucid and vigorous style *can be achieved* if we take the trouble to correct certain failings.

Exercise 4
Change the passive to the active voice in the following sentences:

1 It was noted by the enquiry group that some of the information had been found to be unreliable.
2 The cost of the new project was underestimated by the planners, and the development of the scheme has now been taken over by a newly constituted committee.
3 A huge repast was partaken of by everyone present.
4 A great deal of effort, time, and money are saved by this method.
5 A charming and intelligent performance was given by this new young actress.

Diction: misused words

Misuse of a word often arises from its over-use, coupled with a misunderstanding of its exact meaning. The result is writing that is unclear and sometimes meaningless. Meanings do change but for the most part the changes are slow and it takes a long time for a new meaning to become established and accepted. The exercises in this section draw attention to some words that are often misused, although they have precise meanings.

Have your dictionary to hand when you do the exercises.

Exercise 5

Below are pairs of sentences. Each pair provides a correct and an incorrect use of a word. For each pair:

● say which sentence uses the word *correctly*;

● say what is *wrong* about its use in the incorrect sentence.

Use a dictionary to help you if necessary:

1 (a) For an hour or two yesterday I had a really chronic headache.
  (b) Through all those years he was always good-tempered and serene, even though he was a chronic invalid.

2 (a) On my desk there is a letter that purports to be written by the key witness of the incident.
  (b) What does she purport to do about so serious a discrepancy in the society's accounts?

3 (a) Wagner is detestable; I'm severely allergic to his music.
  (b) After years of suffering from a hayfever-like irritation he was found to be allergic to the fur of his own pet cat.

4 (a) The chief protagonists in the quarrel were the prime minister and the chancellor of the exchequer.
  (b) In *Hamlet* the foppish Rosencrantz and Guildenstern serve to bring out the more austere characteristics of the princely protagonist.

5 (a) A speedy end to widespread unemployment is crucial for our economy.
  (b) The meeting of the heads of departments to consider the two proposed degree courses will be the crucial one.

6 (a) How does one deal with the dilemma generated by the person who announces, 'I am a liar'?
  (b) He was faced with the dilemma of being unable to pay for the meal he had eaten.

7 (a) A generous gift from an anonymous donor facilitated the whole rescue operation.
  (b) The research student was facilitated by an extremely helpful archivist.

Language maintains its vitality and expressiveness through gradual development and change, so we should not be over-pedantic or over-conservative about meanings and rules. What is important is to know, or to be prepared to find out, the established meanings of words, so that we may be aware not only of misuse but also of developments that enrich and enliven the language. Look out for words that come into fashion through broadcasting and journalism and then become over-used. Check their meanings with a dictionary and then look critically at the uses to which they are being put.

Exercise 6

Below is a list of words that are often used in a very slipshod way. Write down what you think each word means and, if you like, write a short sentence using the word. Look up the meanings of the words in your dictionary, or compare your meanings with those in the answers section.

exotic	viable	trauma
valid	parameter	charisma
echelon	prestigious	disinterested

We often pick up new words from radio and television. This means that we learn the words by hearing rather than by seeing them, and that we often guess or infer their meanings from the context in which they are used. As a result we may be uncertain about spellings and meanings, and may easily confuse similar-looking or similar-sounding words when we eventually see them on the page or come to write them. Once again, the use of a dictionary can save us from error and help us to build up a valuable vocabulary.

Exercise 7

Below are some pairs and trios of similar words. Look up the meanings of any you do not fully understand and then fill the blank in each of the sentences 1–18 with the correct word:

factitious	attrition	garrulous	imminent
fictitious	contrition	gregarious	eminent
			immanent

expiate	deprecate	emigrant	expedient
explicate	depreciate	immigrant	expeditious
expatiate			

1 Because of his _____ nature he found it difficult to study alone in his room.

2 What began as a few sharp exchanges between opposing factions developed into a war of _____.

3 Politicians tend to do something because it is _____ rather than because it is just.

4 The surgeon performing the kidney transplant was the most _____ man in this particular branch of surgery.

5 After a serious accident, the _____ arrival of the ambulance is often the crucial factor in the task of saving life.

6 As the examination became _____, the better-prepared students grew worried; the least-prepared students were openly panicking.

7 At this point he began to _____ on the virtues of his latest invention.

8 In order to _____ his intolerable conduct of the previous evening, he sent his mother a bunch of flowers.

9 The boy was full of _____ for his thoughtless behaviour towards the old man.

10 His dream of silence was shattered by the presence of a _____ hiker who caught him up at the top of the hill.

11 I shall ask him to _____ the complex procedures for obtaining a long-term visa for the USA.

12 Some theologians think of God as quite separate from the universe; others regard him as _____.

13 As soon as one puts a car on the road, its value begins to
   _____.

14 A person who emigrates from his home country is called an
   _____.

15 He came to the conclusion that the whole incident was con-
   trived and that even her declared concern and anxiety were
   _____.

16 Over-modest persons often _____ any praise they are
   offered.

17 A person coming into a country to settle there is called an
   _____.

18 All the characters in my novel are _____.

Ornate writing

The essence of good style is clarity and precision. This does
not mean that long words, technical terms, and detailed
descriptions are never needed in academic writing. But high-
flown phrases and a needless profusion of long words,
although they may sometimes give a superficial impression
of expertise, are never in themselves good style. When an
idea can be clearly and adequately expressed in simple
words, then simple words should be used. For instance, the
instruction

A code name should be allotted to each participant

becomes clearer, more direct, and more vigorous when
expressed as

Give everyone a code name.

The exercises in this section will show, and ask you to
correct, a range of bad practices that produce over-elaborate,
recondite writing.

Exercise 8

Rewrite the sentences below, making them clear without loss of meaning:

1 The match had to be postponed because of the unfavourable climatic conditions.
2 Continual vigilance is essential in this matter.
3 We shall have to implement procedures for converting the buildings for residential purposes.
4 Can you supply us with the requisite information concerning the causes of the present difficulty?
5 Let us commence by extending our warmest felicitations to our new president.
6 Few applicants understood the requirements of the employment, and in some cases were entirely lacking in suitable qualifications.

Style is often weakened by sentences that are unnecessarily repetitive. A *redundant* word is one that is superfluous because it more or less repeats the meaning of another word already used in the sentence:

Throughout his entire reign, the king ignored his favourite's despicable conduct.

In that sentence, 'entire' is redundant. Its work has already been done by 'throughout'. All that is needed for the opening phrase is

Throughout his reign ...

Exercise 9

Correct the redundancies in the following:

1 The consequent results were ...
2 At this moment in time ...
3 What are the important essentials?
4 I was acting hastily on an impulse.

5 Is it within the realm of possibility?
6 Let's hope that they will not prejudge him in advance.
7 She still continued to complain.
8 The companies could merge together to form a large syndicate.
9 The subject of the talk is about our recent economic recovery.
10 The reason for the delay was because of his illness.
11 It seems apparent to me that ...
12 The greater majority wanted to accept the offer.

Redundancy is not the only kind of repetition that can mar writing. An unnecessary repetition of a word already used generally produces a clumsy effect and gives the impression of muddled thought:

Because Jason had dealt so summarily with Millie yesterday, because of his anxiety over the lost necklace, he was now eager to heal the wounds he had inflicted on their friendship.

Sometimes, the repetition of a *sound* creates a slightly ludicrous effect:

His calculation proved to be a precise evaluation of the situation.

Exercise 10

All the sentences below are examples of ornate writing of various kinds. Write an improved version of each sentence:

1 It would be more preferable to await the resulting consequences of this mutual co-operation.
2 We are now in a position to make you an offer of employment on a part-time basis.
3 She was seen driving a blue coloured car down the main street.
4 Do be sure to give sufficient consideration to the matter before taking action on the issue.
5 The new tower block will certainly be detrimental to the visual amenities of the surrounding district.

6 Mr Thomas had just retired for the night when he remembered that there was a shortfall in supplies of paperclips at the office.

Exercise 11

In the paragraph below, underline the words and phrases that make it unnecessarily elaborate. Write an improved version of the paragraph.

When a second-hand car is being purchased, you should examine it with a considerable amount of care. The driving seat should be given particular attention. The reason for this is because a car that has been subjected to a great deal of use will, in all probability, have a badly worn driving seat. In the majority of instances the person selling the car will have touched-up the spots of rust that were on the body of the car. A finger should therefore be run cautiously along the lower rim of the chassis in order to detect hidden and untreated rust. As a result, you may then find yourself in a very favourable bargaining position.

This section has emphasised clarity, precision, and brevity as essential elements of a good academic style. But please remember the point made in the introduction to the chapter: there is no one 'good style' that is suitable for every kind of writing. A piece of writing should have a style that is appropriate to the work it does.

Jargon

The word *jargon* once meant 'the babbling of birds'. Nowadays it is used to refer to talk that sounds ugly and is difficult to understand. In particular it refers to that mass of technical language from the sciences, business, industry, the social sciences, technology, and the trades and professions, that unceasingly invades the less-specialised world of ordinary writing and talking.

It isn't difficult to cultivate a sensitive eye and ear for jargon, for its use is widespread on radio and television and in newspapers and magazines. It flourishes in the company of clichés, redundancies, misused words, and all kinds of verbosity and vagueness. In its proper place, jargon is simply convenient technical terminology invented by specialists for their own use; but if allowed to be busy away from home it can quickly become gibberish. Its pomposity can move us to laughter, its meaninglessness to rage, its wrongheaded ingenuity to amazement and despair.

Below is an example of jargon run wild. It comes from a social services report and was quoted in a letter to the *Guardian* on 18 January 1978.

This elderly geriatric female has multiple joint problems which limit perambulation. Absence of verbal intercourse aggravates her detachment from reality and reinforces isolationism. She is unable to relate to events at this point in time. Psychogeriatric consider-ation in the context of conceptual distortion and paranoia is also a parameter in the total dimension of her problems.

Cited by Dwight Bolinger in 'Fire in a Wooden Stove', in
L. Michaels and P. Ricks, eds, *The State of the Language*, p. 385

That passage is a mixture of technical terms taken from medicine ('geriatric', 'psychogeriatric', 'paranoia'), and un-necessarily pompous expressions ('limit perambulation', 'verbal intercourse', 'conceptual distortion'). It is a clear example of the kind of stylistic failings we shall be looking at in this section's exercises.

Exercise 12
Write a clearer, simpler version of the quoted passage above.

Exercise 13
In the sentences below, underline the jargon terms and any other phrases that you think could be improved:

1 I feel it is incumbent upon me to point out that we are operating with a low manpower ceiling.
2 He is undertaking a study of teacher–child communication inter-actions in a controlled classroom environment.
3 This vegetable protein substitute for meat is indistinguishable from the real thing when placed in a gravy situation.
4 The process has been developed in recognition of the changing socio-economic patterns of contemporary society.

Journalism has a jargon so familiar to most of us that it is almost indistinguishable from our common stock of every-day clichés. We rarely pause to question the style of phrases such as 'it was learned that' or 'he received a severe head wound'. Good journalistic writing should impact immedi-ately; it should be vivid and concise without being sen-sational. Yet it is so often dull and confused, using abstract words where particular ones would bring a piece of infor-mation to life, and using technical terms where everyday language could do a better job.

Exercise 14
Rewrite the sentences below to make them more concise and direct:

1 There has been a considerable deterioration in the High Street traffic situation.
2 The youths made good their escape down a rear alley.
3 Their travel arrangements were in the hands of the chairman's secretary.
4 The council has decided to augment the grant provision for the domestic accommodation improvement programme.
5 Over the past twelve months there has been a decrease in the rate of the depletion of oil supplies.

Exercise 15

The paragraph below is my own invention but it is written in a style that must be familiar to everyone. Underline the words and phrases that make the writing stale and trite. Can you say exactly what it is that gives this style its characteristic tone?

An acute dilemma today confronts the tight-knit little community of the sun-baked island of San Juliano. The romantic desert island's main street is strangely desolate and an eerie silence lies over the scattering of houses that straggle up the steep hillside behind the idyllic shoreline. In San Juliano's tiny primitive meeting-house sit ten grim-faced and silent men, their eyes fixed on the small intricately carved box that stands on the rough wooden table in the middle of the room.

Vocabulary

So far, in this chapter, the main emphasis has been on the work of correcting over-elaborate writing by using simpler words and excising unnecessary ones. But the advantages of possessing a large vocabulary must not be overlooked. Using a large vocabulary does not go against the general principles of simplicity and clarity.

One obvious advantage of a large vocabulary is that it helps us to think and to express ourselves precisely. Another is that it increases our understanding and critical appreciation of what we read. Some people think that any use of long, unusual, difficult, or technical words is either one-upmanship, pedantry, or insensitiveness to the ordinary standards of writing and conversation. That, to me, seems a superficial view which, if acted upon, would not only diminish the sensitivity and richness of the language, but would also destroy the whole idea of the enjoyment and exploration of the meanings and sounds of words. Simple words cannot do *all* the work that language has to do. If we remember that the style of a piece of writing should be appropriate to the job it is meant to do, and that simple words should be used if they are able to do all that the job requires, then we should not find ourselves using difficult or unusual words in the wrong places.

At several points in this book I have had to think very carefully about whether to use some slightly unusual word that has come to mind. On p. 89 I hesitated for some time before using the word 'recondite'. How well known was it? Would it put off the reader who didn't know its meaning? Was there a less unusual word that would do just as well? In the end I decided I would use it. It was, I argued, an expressive, succinct word that said exactly what I wanted to say. My use of it would invite any reader to whom it was new to take the lesson of my book to heart and find the word in a dictionary. And it would make a useful addition to any such reader's vocabulary.

The exercises in this section concentrate on the meanings of slightly unusual words that are nevertheless useful and expressive.

The names of well-known heroes of mythology and famous historical persons are sometimes turned into adjectives. This is done by putting a suitable ending on the name and changing the name's capital letter into a small letter. For example, a task demanding great physical strength and prowess is sometimes described as 'a herculean labour'. In that phrase the adjective *herculean* derives from the name Hercules. Hercules was a Greek hero who was famous for his exploits and his Twelve Labours, in which his strength and courage were unsurpassed.

Exercise 16
Write the meanings of the words that are italicised in the sentences below, using a dictionary to help you if necessary:

1 Any president of the USA faces a challenge that demands ability and vision of *promethean* magnitude.

2 He was a quiet, contented man who was modestly *epicurean* in his private life.

3 The rain lashed our faces and a gale of *titanic* force suddenly seized at the mainsail.

4 Our school system seems to provide a somewhat *procrustean* environment for some of our more talented children.

5 Throughout this long period of adversity he retained his *stoical* attitude.

6 He had an almost *protean* capacity for meeting every fresh difficulty that confronted him in his work to establish the new university.

7 When the present government came to power, *draconian* measures were introduced.

Exercise 17

This exercise gives you practice in using the words we have already looked at in exercise 16 (herculean, promethean, protean, procrustean, draconian, epicurean, stoical, titanic).

Write the correct word in the gap in each of the following sentences:

1 Her ingenuity was amazing; she had a magical and quite _____ adaptability.

2 It was a job for a superman, someone with _____ powers.

3 The enormous palace seemed to be built for inhabitants of _____ proportions.

4 He finally decided that he would reject the values of his past life and cultivate only _____ pleasures.

5 Suddenly she saw the whole enterprise for what it was: a life's work, offering _____ rewards and suffering.

6 It was a gruelling trial and everyone present came to respect the prisoner's _____ calm.

7 We have striven all these years to produce this organisation, only to find we have made ourselves a _____ bed.

8 During a national crisis people are more ready to accept legislation of a _____ type.

In Fowler's *Modern English Usage*, there is an entry headed 'slipshod extension'. Slipshod extension occurs when the meaning of a word is stretched beyond its proper application. The word *feasible* is an example of this. *Feasible* means 'capable of being done', but it is often incorrectly extended to mean 'possible'. The two words are certainly not synonymous; as Fowler points out, a thunderstorm is *possible*, but not *feasible*.

The next exercise concentrates on words whose meanings are often extended or misapplied in this kind of way.

Exercise 18
Write what you think are the meanings of the words and phrases below. Check your answers with a dictionary and also with my answers and comments:

1 *oblivious* of
2 to *refute*
3 it *transpired* that
4 a *discrete* entity
5 *mitigating* circumstances
6 an *alibi*

Exercise 19
Tick the sentences below that use the italicised words correctly. Correct the faulty sentences:

1 The information we have just been given is bound to *mitigate against* his case.
2 The counselling service must be linked to other departments: it will be of no use as a *discrete* entity.
3 She seemed *oblivious* to what was going on around her.
4 I utterly *refute* your allegations.
5 His *alibi* is that he was interviewing a cabinet minister in London at the time of the Liverpool murder.
6 Both chess players were in excellent form for what *transpired* to be the last game in the congress.

You may like to check the meanings of the words listed below and then keep yourself alert to their daily use in newspapers and conversation, and on the radio and television.

hopefully	facilitate	decimate	situation	cohort
credibility	credulity	paradigm	derisory	flaunt
flout	trauma	alternative	involve	catalyst

Revision exercises

Use your dictionary and refer back to earlier sections when necessary.

Exercise 20
Write improved versions of the following sentences:

1 It was noted by the investigators that stress behaviour was exhibited by at least one third of the tested rats.
2 Without a shadow of doubt, we should clearly declare our intentions for the immediate future.
3 His support is crucial to the scheme we have chosen.
4 Ford's new model has been subjected to stringent tests and will soon be available to purchasers nationwide.
5 A specimen paper was prepared by three members of the examination board.

Exercise 21
Tick the sentences that use the italicised words correctly. Correct those that use them wrongly:

1 He has not ridden a horse for many years as he has been *chronically* ill.
2 I am really *allergic* to light romantic novels.
3 Who is to be the chief *protagonist* in this venture?
4 She hopes that her research programme will be *facilitated* by an educational trust.

5 In *anticipation* of a terrorist attack they arranged for a bullet-proof car to take the diplomat to the airport.

Exercise 22
Write the meanings of the following words:

exotic	parameter
echelon	charisma
viable	disinterested

Exercise 23
Cross out the incorrect word in the sentences below:

1 She has decided to immigrate/emigrate from her home country.
2 He is a distinguished academic and an eminent/imminent politician.
3 When a conflict between two nations is particularly bitter, it is often spoken of as 'a war of attrition/contrition'.
4 As a child I was not talkative, but my brother, in contrast, was extremely gregarious/garrulous.
5 Please could you expiate/explicate these instructions for me?

Exercise 24
Rewrite the sentences below to make them clearer and simpler:

1 The committee has the recruitment situation under active consideration at the present moment.
2 If enrolment is successful in terms of numbers, then we shall be able to implement a reduction in fees.
3 The 1980s will probably call for a continuing development of flexible and facilitative arrangements for crêche facilities and maternity and paternity leave provision.

Exercise 25
What are the following?

1 a protean ability
2 a stoical attitude
3 a procrustean bed
4 draconian measures
5 epicurean tastes
6 promethean prospects
7 titanic proportions
8 herculean power

Exercise 26
Cross out the incorrect words in the sentences below:

1 When engrossed in his work he was entirely oblivious/unaware of the noises around him.
2 Her alibi/excuse was that she had a severe headache at home-work time.
3 She intends to offer a sound argument that will refute/deny his allegations.
4 What transpired/happened next was that he produced a gun and fired a shot at the locked door.

6 Academic apparatus

Some Latin terms and their abbreviations
Latin terms again   Bibliographies for books and articles
References and footnotes in books and articles
A method for essays; abbreviations; some Latin phrases
Revision exercises

This chapter deals with some of the main conventions and techniques for the scholarly presentation of written work. Use or quotation of other people's ideas or words in your essays must always be acknowledged, and there are various conventions for making such acknowledgements and citing sources; you will quickly come across some of them if you glance through two or three text books or collections of papers. Some books give footnotes and references on the pages to which they apply; others give them at the ends of chapters or sections, or at the end of the book. Some books use Latin abbreviations and terms in their footnotes; others avoid them if they can. But whatever arrangements or conventions are chosen, the aim is always to supply complete information about sources in as concise a way as possible. When you write an essay, you should have the same aim.

    The chapter provides a working knowledge of the main terms, abbreviations, and conventions used for citing sources. From the information given, and from the examples and exercises, you should be able to choose a method which suits your own work. Knowledge of a range of conventions should help you to present your written work in a scholarly way and gain a fuller understanding of what you read.

The chapter begins by looking at a few Latin abbreviations that are used not only in footnotes but also, from time to time, in the main text of books and essays. It then deals with the conventions for bibliographies and reference footnotes and, finally, with a further range of abbreviations and Latin terms.

Some Latin terms and their abbreviations

There is nothing greatly superior about Latin terms but their use is well established and you will probably come across them often in your reading, usually in abbreviated forms. It's as well therefore to know the meanings of the most-used Latin terms so that you understand them when you read them, even though you may prefer not to use them in your own work.

Only four abbreviated Latin terms are widely used in the main text of books and essays. They are 'e.g.', 'i.e.', 'etc.', and 'viz.'. The use of most other Latin abbreviations is generally confined to footnotes.

Exercise 1

The four most-used abbreviated Latin terms are listed below. See if you can write the English meaning of each in the middle column of the chart. Try the 'full Latin' column as well if you wish, although it isn't necessary to know the full Latin in order to understand or use the abbreviations:

Latin abbreviation	English meaning	Full Latin
e.g.		
i.e.		
etc.		
viz.		

Answers for Chapter 6 are on pp. 204–9.

Exercise 2

In the following sentences write in the brackets provided the English meanings of the Latin abbreviations:

1 The good historian uses a wide range of sources: letters, documents, official records, diaries, etc. (   )

2 It is not enough for the historian to concern himself simply with assembling material, i.e. (   ) he is not a mere collector of data.

3 He has also to make certain judgements about his sources, e.g. (   ) whether a particular writer might have given a biased account of an event.

4 Moreover, the historian needs an understanding of the diversity and richness of human ideas, and for this understanding there is one major requirement, viz. (   ) a broad-based, liberal education.

It's important to understand that 'i.e.' (*id est* = that is) and 'e.g.' (*exempli gratia* = for example) are not interchangeable. 'e.g.' precedes the *giving of an example or examples*:

We need to be given more details of the incident, e.g. whether there were any chance visitors in the area who might have seen the attack.

'i.e.' introduces *another way of saying* what has already been said, driving home a point already made:

Do not use the components from this sealed box until absolutely necessary, i.e. when all the other components have been used.

Nor are 'i.e.' and 'viz.' (*videlicet* = namely) interchangeable. 'i.e.' *paraphrases* something already said, but 'viz.' *specifies*, or *names*, or *makes particular* something already mentioned in general terms:

There was one cause to which he gave total allegiance and most of his money, viz. the furtherance of the teaching of the Cornish language.

Exercise 3

Write the correct Latin abbreviations (either e.g., i.e., etc., or viz.) in the following sentences:

1 Some of the old names, _____ 'maslin' for mixed corn, and 'reeke' for hayrick, are almost forgotten.
2 He had to confess to having only one source of income, _____ a weekly rent paid to him by a neighbour for the use of the garage.
3 If we are to take action we need proof of his having been one of the defaulters, _____ we need clear evidence of his guilt.
4 Her book purports to examine all the ingredients of our national lethargy: our greed, arrogance, indolence, _____.

There are two other Latin abbreviations which occasionally occur in the main text, as well as in the footnotes, of books and essays. They are:

● c. (*circa*) = about, or around (a date or year):

A small group of English lawyers began to make their living from the practice of civil rather than common law c. 1620.

● v. (*vide*) = see:

The question of what it is that periodically generates a craze for witchcraft must be considered more carefully (v. chapter five in this book), once its historical origins have been investigated.

Exercise 4

Fill the gaps in the chart below. Treat the 'full Latin' column as optional, if you wish:

Latin abbreviation	English meaning	Full Latin
etc.		
	that is	
		videlicet
	for example	
c		
		vide

Latin terms again

The exercises below should help to increase your familiarity with the Latin phrases already encountered in the previous section. Before starting the exercises, look again at the chart on p. 204, and remind yourself of the differences pointed out between i.e., e.g., and viz.

Exercise 5

In the following sentences:

- underline the words that can be replaced by Latin terms;
- write the appropriate Latin abbreviation in the bracket at the end of each sentence.

1 A trauma or traumatic experience is something that is not only distressing at the time, but also has lasting pathological effects, that is, it is a wound which leaves scars. ( )

2 Freud described certain techniques of the ego, for example, repression, projection, and reaction-formation, as 'defence-mechanisms'. ( )

3 'Anti-psychiatry' became an influential movement in the 1960s and is now under severe critical scrutiny; see Cooper, D., 'The anti-hospital: an experiment in psychiatry', *New Society*, 11 March 1965, 5, No. 128. ( )

4 According to Freud, maturation consists in passing through a series of phases which are related to the physical sources of erotic pleasure, namely, the oral, anal, and phallic. ( )

5 Treatment producing fits in patients actually worked best with those patients who had been misdiagnosed, that is, those who were not schizophrenic at all. ( )

6 Epidemiology, a method of tracing the sources of an outbreak of a disease, was of course unknown at the time of the scourge of plagues that erupted in Europe in about 1390. ( )

Exercise 6

In the following:

● tick the sentences which use Latin abbreviations correctly;
● correct the sentences which use Latin phrases wrongly.

1 He once told me an enthralling story c. his grandmother's involvement in the revolution.

2 She frequently lavished presents on the most unlikely people, i.e. on the baker, and on a girl she met only once in the public library.

3 He began to spend about twelve hours each day in the laboratory, working on what was to become his ruling interest, viz. bacterial action on the carbon compounds of plant systems.

4 John Samuel Pettigrew is known to have lived in Wiltshire for most of his life and one reliable source mentions that he was born near Malmesbury c. 1646.

5 Uniformitarians maintain that the world is the product of a basic set of forces (e.g. natural selection) working slowly over a period of time.

6 It is well known that Jesus said, 'Suffer (i.e. allow) the little children to come unto me.'

7 Phobic states can arise in almost any connexion and can be about very ordinary things, viz., doors, dogs, bridges, cats.

Exercise 7

In each of the following:

● insert the appropriate Latin abbreviation in the space;
● write the English meaning in the bracket at the end of the sentence.

1 He will not be attending the ceremony for a very good reason, _____ that he has not been invited. (   )

2 Some words, _____ army, fleet, government, party, majority, stand either for an individual entity or for a composite group. (   )

3 In large businesses, computers are extensively used to deal with repetitive and routine tasks, _____ the lower-level clerical work. (   )

4 Hyphens can be extremely important (_____ Partridge's *Usage and Abusage*, p. 146), as one realises in reflecting on the differences in meaning between 'he was an Indian fighter' and 'he was an Indian-fighter'. (   )

5 God's omniscience and man's freedom may be endlessly debated (_____ the superb discussion in A. N. Prior's *Formal Logic*, part III, ch. II, sect. 2). (   )

6 George Watson instructs us never to capitalise, _____ put entire words into capital letters, when citing the titles of books used as sources. (   )

Exercise 8
Fill in the gaps in the chart below. Again treat the 'full Latin' column as optional if you wish:

Latin abbreviation	English meaning	Full Latin
		exempli gratia
i.e.		
	about, around	
		et cetera
viz.		
	see	

Bibliographies for books and articles

Most scholarly books, papers, and articles have bibliographies. A well-presented student essay should also have one.

Exercise 9
Write down very briefly what you think a bibliography is and say why scholarly writings have bibliographies. Use a dictionary to help you if you wish.

There is not one accepted form for the presentation of bibliographic information. A glance at several text books will quickly show you a whole range of possible variations. We shall look first at a basic method that is widely used for describing books and papers.

A bibliographic description for a book may be given in the following way:

- author's (or editor's) surname, followed by forename or initials;
- title, *underlined*;
- publisher and date of publication, in brackets (*or* place and date of publication); e.g.

Gowers, Ernest, The Complete Plain Words (Penguin, 1973)

It is important that the items of information are given in the order listed above. Note that the book title, when written, is always underlined. In print it appears in italics. Details of a book's publisher and date of publication are usually found somewhere on its first three or four pages.

Exercise 10

Take two of your own books and write their descriptions as for a bibliography. Check your descriptions against the list above to make sure you have the items in the correct order.

A method for providing bibliographic information for a course-work essay will be suggested late in this chapter.

Bibliographic descriptions of papers and articles give details in the same order as for books. The title of a paper or article is *not* underlined but placed between single quotation marks. The name of the journal, periodical, or book containing the paper *is underlined*. A bibliographic description for a paper or article requires:

- author's name, followed by forename or initials;
- title of paper in *single quotation marks*;
- name of journal or book containing article, *underlined*;
- number of volume or issue;
- date of publication, in brackets; e.g.

Trilling, L., 'In Mansfield Park', <u>Encounter</u>, 3, No. 3 (Sept. 1954)

Exercise 11

Write an entry for a bibliography for each of the books or papers described in 1–4 below:

1 I was reading a paper by J. D. Dimmick the other day, published in June 1923. It is in the no. 6 issue of <u>Politics for People</u> and its title is 'Pragmatism and Principles: a Common-sense View'.

2 There's an excellent book which was published by the Rapier Press in 1966, called <u>English Country Customs</u>. The author is W. J. Seldon.

3 If you can get hold of volume 17, issue number 2, of the <u>British Journal of Aesthetics,</u> you'll find the article I mentioned by T. J. Diffey, called 'The Idea of Art'. That particular volume came out in spring 1977.

4 J. R. Miller has edited a comprehensive survey of computer systems of the nineteen-seventies. It was published in 1980 by Macdonald's under the title <u>A Decade of Computer Systems.</u>

You may already have noticed and picked up the system of punctuation I have been using for bibliographic descriptions. Once again the aim is to achieve complete clarity without unnecessary fuss. In the main, commas are used to mark off the separate details of the information. The basic pattern for punctuation is as follows:

- author's (or editor's) surname, comma;
- initials (with stops),
- or first name, comma;
- title;

- opening bracket, name of publisher, comma, date, closing bracket.

Notice that:

- in a bibliography in list form, there is no final stop after each entry;
- in an alphabetically presented bibliography the initial letter of the *surname* of the author or editor governs the alphabetical position of each item.

References and footnotes in books and articles

Whether you are writing a course essay, a dissertation, a paper, a thesis, or a book, all references in it to the ideas or words of other people must be acknowledged, and their sources given. In this section we shall look at some of the conventions used for supplying footnotes for published writings and for dissertations, papers, and essays that are to be formally presented. The next section will then outline a method for combining references and bibliographic information that is suitable for course-work essays. In what follows I shall refer mostly to books but what I say applies also to other published or formally presented writing.

In a book a reference is usually given in a footnote. The reference footnote supplies information that enables the reader to find *exactly* the place in the source referred to by the author. Footnote numbers may begin either with '1' on each page or they may run consecutively from the beginning to the end of a chapter, or even from beginning to end of a whole book. The footnote numeral is placed at the end of the matter to which it refers and the footnote itself, preceded by its number, is then placed at the foot of the page. (When there are very few footnotes it is common practice to use symbols such as the asterisk, used on p. 63 of this book.)

When a book or article has a bibliography full publication details of a source need not be given in its footnotes. The following information is sufficient:

- author or editor's name, with first name or initials first;
- title of book (underlined), or article (in single quotation marks);
- page or pages referred to; e.g.

[1] Adrian G. Drew, <u>Seventeenth-Century Science</u>, pp. 72–75.
[2] H. Adam, 'A New Economic Strategy', p. 18.

Have you noticed the differences between the way in which a footnote reference is given and the way in which a bibliographic entry is given? Glance back to p. 109 so that you can compare the two, and note down the differences. They may seem rather trivial and unnecessary, but there are reasons for them. The differences are:

- In a reference footnote, the author's or editor's *initials or first name* are placed first; in a bibliography, the author's or editor's *surname* is placed first.
- In a reference footnote, pages are cited; in a bibliography, they are not.
- A reference footnote ends with a stop; a bibliographic entry does not.

These differences of form relate to the different purposes of bibliographies and reference footnotes. The purpose of a bibliographic description is to enable the reader to identify precisely the *work* that has been referred to or quoted. The purpose of a reference footnote is to enable the reader to find *a specific part* of a work. In a bibliographic entry the author's name is placed first because its initial letter governs its place in the alphabetical order. In a reference footnote, a page number or numbers must be given so that the exact part of the work cited may be easily found. A full stop is needed at the end of a reference footnote as further sentences of comment or information may follow it.

Exercise 12

The passage below mentions a remark which occurs on p. 152 of a book called *Themes and Episodes*, published in 1966 in New York and written by Igor Stravinsky and Robert Craft. Insert a footnote numeral at the appropriate point in the passage and write:

● a reference footnote for it; and
● a bibliographic description for it.

In one of Igor Stravinsky's less charitable conversations he talks of 'a worthy woman who naturally and unfortunately looked irate, like a hen, even when in good humour.' One may quarrel whether hens look irate, maybe peevish would be a better word here, but no one would easily deny that they have an 'expression' which an unfortunate woman may share.

The form of a reference footnote about a paper or article varies only slightly from that for a book. It requires:

● name of author, with first name or initials first;
● title of article, *in single quotation marks*;
● page numbers; e.g.

Graham McFee, 'The Fraudulent in Art', p. 222.

Exercise 13

The passage below refers to an article which appeared in *Encounter*, vol. xxviii, no. 1, January 1967. The article is called 'The Sanctity of Life' and was written by Edward Shils. Insert a footnote numeral at an appropriate point in the passage, and write:

● a reference footnote for it; and
● a bibliographic description for it.

Although religious belief is in decline, there are still many people who experience a deep revulsion at the thought of genetic tampering. The origins of this revulsion are questioned in an article by Edward Shils. Is it, he asks, simply a vestigial feeling left over from earlier beliefs?

After a first reference to a work subsequent references may be made in a short form which gives only the author's last name and a page reference, e.g.

Drew, p. 84.

If there is no possibility of ambiguity, then it is sufficient to give just the page reference in brackets in the text.

Another method is to use the Latin abbreviation 'ibid.' in the footnote (*ibidem* = in the same place). 'ibid.' is used only when references to the same work follow each other with no intervening reference or references to other works. It stands for *all* the items of the preceding reference *except* the page number. Thus, if the reference is to exactly the same passage as previously cited, then 'ibid.' alone is enough; but if the reference is to a different page or pages, then the new page number(s) must be given, e.g.

[1] Adrian G. Drew, *Seventeenth-Century Science*, pp. 72–75.
[2] ibid., p. 94.

If you have come across 'ibid.' in footnotes you have probably also noticed two other Latin abbreviations, 'op. cit.', and 'loc. cit.'. Although there is a gradual decline in the use of these terms and a gradual increase in the use of English words, you should know what the terms signify when they occur in footnotes:

op. cit. is an abbreviation of *opere citato* = in the work cited;
loc. cit. is an abbreviation of *loco citato* = in the place cited.

'op. cit.' refers us only to the *work* already cited; so in order to make the reference specific it must be accompanied by page or chapter numbers. 'loc. cit.' refers to *the same place* in a work as that given in the previous citation.

Confusions can arise if these Latin abbreviations are used carelessly. You should know their meanings but for your own use I recommend the simpler method used in the first example on p. 114 for making references that follow after the first reference.

The sciences and social sciences have developed their own conventions for making references. One fairly common practice in the social sciences is as follows: No footnotes are provided. Instead, brief references consisting simply of the author's surname and the publication date of his work are placed within brackets *in the main text*, e.g.

An analysis of the data collected from the whole series of experiments was provided (Smithson, 1979).

Or, if the author's name occurs *in the sentence*, then only the year of publication is given, e.g.

Smithson provided an anlysis of the data he had collected from the whole series of experiments (1979).

Full details for all the references are then listed in an alphabetical reference bibliography at the end of the book, or in separate reference bibliographies at the ends of chapters. The reference bibliography combines the functions of reference footnotes and bibliography in one list. In it, the name of the publisher is given as well as the place of publication. The requirements for this kind of bibliographic entry are as follows:

- author's or editor's surname, followed by first name or initials;
- year of publication, in brackets;
- title of book (underlined); or of article (in single

quotation marks) with name of journal (underlined), volume number, etc.;
- place of publication and publisher;
- chapter or page number(s) of cited passage; e.g.

Aron, R. (1969), <u>Main Currents in Sociological Thought</u>, Harmondsworth, Penguin Books, pp. 20–26

An even simpler method, used mainly in scientific writing, is to place a numeral in brackets immediately after a mention of or quotation from a work, and then to give the full reference, against the number, in a reference bibliography at the end of the book, e.g.

In the mid-seventies, Patterson did a great deal to present the whole spectrum of problems about nuclear power to the layman (1).

Exercise 14

Write bibliographic descriptions, using the form given in the preceding paragraph, from the information given below:

1 Harvard University Press brought out, at Harvard in 1968, a book by F. Manuel called <u>A Portrait of Isaac Newton</u>, and the passage I am recommending to you is on pp. 9, 10.
2 E. Nagel's <u>The Structure of Science</u> was published in London by Routledge in 1961.
3 I'd like to refer you to chapter four of Max Weber's <u>The Methodology of the Social Sciences</u> in the edition published by the Free Press, Chicago, in 1957.

A method for essays; abbreviations; some Latin phrases

The conventions outlined in the previous section present a rather bewildering range of methods from which to choose one for your own use in ordinary course-work essays. What is needed is a method that is both clear and economical. In the first part of this section I shall suggest one that combines reference footnotes and bibliography, and that also allows for notes that comment on, or give further information about, points made in your main text. The second part of the section looks at abbreviations used to make these kinds of notes as concise as possible, and also at some Latin phrases you may encounter in your reading.

A simple and clear way of combining references and bibliography and of providing comments on your main text is as follows:

- number your references, and any matter requiring comment, consecutively through your essay;
- at the end of the essay, under the heading 'Notes', give the appropriate information against each number, combining reference details with full bibliographic information. I suggest giving the publisher's name rather than the place of a work's publication; e.g.

1 J. T. Trillingham, *Mediaeval Sorcery* (Axworth Books, 1976), p. 22.

Exercise 15
Write bibliographic/reference notes, using the pattern illustrated above, based on the information given in 1, 2, and 3 below.

1 Pan Books published in 1974 an extremely interesting book by J. Cott, called *Stockhausen: Conversations with the Composer*, and the quoted passage occurs on p. 47.
2 The article by E. Ashby, entitled 'Towards an Environmental Ethic', first appeared in *Nature*, 262, in 1976, on pages 84–85.
3 In 1940, Cassell brought out a book by S. Sweig, translated by P. and T. Blewitt, called *Beware of Pity*.

From our survey of a range of conventions for references and notes you should be able to choose or devise a method that will suit your own essays and satisfy the tutors who read them. You may like to consult your tutor about a suitable method, as some colleges and universities lay down their own rules. Whatever method or convention you use, it is important that you use it in an absolutely consistent way throughout an essay or piece of written work.

We come now to the abbreviations used in notes and footnotes. With the exceptions of e.g., i.e., etc., and viz., which we have looked at in the first section of this chapter, abbreviations are not generally used in the main text of an essay. Their chief use is in notes, references, and bibliographies, which they help to make brief and concise.

Exercise 16

Below are listed the more common abbreviations used in notes. Write the full versions of the abbreviations or, in the case of Latin ones, their English meanings.

MS., MSS	ed., eds
p., pp.	fig., figs
l., ll.	trans. (or tr.)
f., ff.	et al.
v.	no., nos
ch., chs	para., paras
vol., vols	cp.

There is a simple rule that governs the punctuation of abbreviations. If the abbreviated or contracted form of the word ends with *the same letter* as the full form, including plurals, it is not given a full stop:

vols paras figs Dr Mrs nos

Abbreviated words that do not end with the same letter as the full form are given a stop:

p. f. no. para. ed. Esq.

Exercise 17

In the sentences below:

- underline words and phrases which may be abbreviated;
- write the abbreviations, punctuating them correctly.

1 This piece of research was not completed because page 102 of the manuscript was missing and no further manuscripts could be traced.
2 In *Critical Appraisals*, volume I, chapters 4 and 5 are devoted to a rebuttal of the objections made by Cooper and James.
3 The first two paragraphs of page 10 relate to figures 1, 2 and 3; lines 12–16 of the third paragraph refer only to figure 4.
4 For a fuller discussion, see H. Leach and H. J. Crane, editors, *Readings in Social Psychology* (Hyam's Press, 1980), volume 4, pages 42–79, page 83, and those following it.

Latin phrases and words are sometimes encountered in the main texts of books and papers. Their use, along with that of Latin abbreviations, is diminishing but they are still part of the stock-in-trade of many writers and you should know the meanings of the most common ones even though you may prefer not to use them yourself. Latin words, like most foreign words, should be underlined. In print they appear in italics.

Exercise 18

Below are the *English meanings* of six Latin phrases or terms and also six sentences, each of which uses one of the Latin terms. For each sentence, write in the brackets provided the

English meaning of the Latin term it uses. Try to puzzle out the meanings of any of which you are uncertain.

| as | in itself | for this particular purpose |
| so, thus | the reverse | to infinity |

1 Once we start asking for the causes of things, we have started an enquiry that can continue *ad infinitum*. (   )
2 We can value something for its use or function, and we can value it *per se*. (   )
3 Should the nuclear scientist, *qua* scientist, be concerned with the uses to which his discoveries might be put? (   )
4 He said that psychology was a subject in which he was 'wholly disinterested' (*sic*). (   )
5 This has been a difficult legal problem, for the woman blames her husband, and *vice versa*. (   )
6 We shall have to abandon all the standard procedures and treat the case in an *ad hoc* way. (   )

Revision exercises

These exercises are not intended simply as memory tests. You should use them to consolidate and revise, that is, to 're-see', the material of the chapter. The most useful way of tackling the exercises is as follows:

● Work through an exercise, doing all you can without referring back.
● Return to any questions you were unsure of, and work them by looking back to the section that dealt with them. Be sure not to skimp the writing out of answers, especially of such things as bibliographic entries and references: it is careful attention to detail at this stage that will help you to learn or correct anything you haven't already mastered.
● Consult the appropriate answers section.

Exercise 19

Insert the appropriate Latin abbreviation in the gap in each of the following sentences:

1 All those who gave generously, _____, contributed at least one half of their earnings, were to be rewarded when the profit-making began.

2 In the nineteenth century Adam Smith pleaded eloquently that all children, at the earliest possible age, should be taught the educational rudiments, _____, reading, writing, and account-ing.

3 Once nature was recognised as a giant mechanism, it became possible to predict natural phenomena, _____, the move-ments of planets and the tides.

4 In the nineteenth century, the term 'factory' covered commercial organisations such as iron-works, dye-works, soap works, brass foundries, _____.

Exercise 20

For each description given below, say whether it is a biblio-graphic entry or a reference footnote (for published or formally presented work):

1 Daniel Defoe, *A Tour Through the Whole Island of Great Britain*, pp. 195–7.

2 Clark, G. N., *Science and Social Welfare in the Age of Newton* (Oxford, 1937)

3 Francis Bacon, 'Of Masques and Triumphs', p. 100.

Exercise 21

In the sentences from essay notes given below,

● underline the words and phrases which may be abbreviated; and

● write the abbreviations, punctuating them correctly.

1 Lines 3–15 on page 22 comprise a passage taken from a manuscript, translated by Edward Bayer, which is discussed in full in chapter 5, page 82 and following pages.

2 A survey conducted by Friedson and others has been reported in three volumes, edited by R. V. Singer.

3 Dawson's theory is mentioned on pages 30, 31 of *Witchcraft*, edited by P. R. Jones (LMP, 1960), and in the closing paragraphs of chapter 10 in the same work.

4 Compare figure 1 on page 2 with figures 8 and 9 on pages 7, 8.

5 Sonata number 10 in the manuscript has four movements; numbers 11 and 12 each have only three.

Exercise 22

Using the information given in 1–3 below, write Notes entries for the end of an essay, combining reference and bibliographic information:

1 This quotation comes from page 80 of Thomas Szasz's book, published by Penguin Books in 1974, called *Ideology and Insanity*.

2 The paper referred to is 'Myth in Theology' by Maurice Wiles, in *The Myth of God Incarnate* edited by John Hick and published in 1977 by SCM Press Ltd.

3 The recommended book is *Introducing James Joyce* by T. S. Eliot, published in 1972 by Faber and Faber.

Exercise 23

Write the appropriate Latin phrase in the blank in each of the sentences 1–5. Remember to underline:

per se = in itself, *qua* = as, *ad hoc* = for this particular purpose, *vice versa* = reversing the positions, *sic* = so, thus, *ad infinitum* = to infinity.

1 The report pointed out that vice-chancellors of universities enjoyed fringe benefits such as the use of a university car and a horse _____.

2 We have looked at all the ramifications of the new proposal, but it is time now to look at the proposal _____.

3 If managers fail to communicate with shop-floor workers, and _____, then inefficiency and discontent are bound to ensue.

4 A work of art, _____ work of art, invokes a special kind of regard from the spectator.

5 The circumstances are so unusual that we shall have to work in an entirely _____ way.

Exercise 24

1 'Translate' the abbreviations in the following notes:

[1] Adrian G. Drew, *Seventeenth-Century Science* (Dobwells, 1975), pp. 22–28.
[2] ibid., p. 84 ff.
[3] The first records of these transactions date from c. 1400.
[4] v. ch. V in this book.
[5] Cp. with Drew, ch. 10.

2 Put stops against the abbreviations requiring them:

para	etc	fig	Esq
chs	Mr	et al	vols
op cit	nos	ll	Mrs

3 What is the difference in purpose between a bibliographic description and a reference footnote?

7 Making notes

Making notes is an important part of the activity of studying. Good notes that are easily understood are the result of
a clear understanding of material and an ability to arrange
its main points in a concise and accurate way. It is worth
taking trouble with notes, for the work of comprehending a
topic and then condensing its content without distortion can
take you a long way towards knowing and learning it.

This chapter presents some techniques for organising
notes and gives you practice in writing them.

Techniques and materials

The best paper for notes is lined, loose-leaf paper of A4 size
that will fit into a ring file. When filed in this way notes may
be added to by inserting extra pages when and where needed.
Different topics may be labelled with stand-up tabs. A wide
right-hand margin is useful for making extra comments,
reminders, or any cross-references and supplements to the
notes.

It is important to decide on a clear system for headings

and numberings. Choose one that suits you and your work and use it consistently. Here is one way of setting out headings and sub-headings for notes on a book:

DEMAND AND SUPPLY   Ralph Turvey

Chapter 1: Consumer Demand (pp. 13–30)

1 The demand for margarine

By ranging from block capitals in the main heading to uncapitalised writing in the chapter sub-heading, I have avoided any underlining in those headings. This means that underlining may be kept for emphasising important points in the notes and will be all the more effective for not being used elsewhere. If the hierarchy of headings is so complex that you *do* need to underline, then remember that several types of underlining are possible: <u>single,</u> <u>double,</u> <u>wavy</u> and <u>broken.</u> Special emphases may be made and relationships between points or sections shown by using colours for underlinings. But be very wary of the over-use of underlinings and colour markings: if too many emphases are made then nothing will stand out as really important.

Exercise 1

Set out the details given in 1–4 below as headings and sub-headings for notes:

1 Aristotle's *Politics* is a work that is arranged in eight books, with several chapters in each book.
2 The William Molesworth edition of Thomas Hobbes's *English Works* comprises several volumes. The first volume, *Elements of Philosophy*, has an opening chapter called 'Of Philosophy'.
3 In his *Cottage Economy*, William Cobbett starts with an important Introduction in which the paragraphs are numbered 1., 2., 3., 4., and so on.
4 The first essay in the collection *Aesthetics and Language*, edited by William Elton, is called 'The Function of Philosophical Aesthetics', and is written by W. B. Gallie.

Answers for Chapter 7 are on pp. 210–15.

There are various numbering systems that are helpful for note-taking: 1, 2, 3; I, II, III; (i), (ii), (iii); A, B, C; a, b, c; 1.1, 1.2, 1.3; 1.11, 1.12, 1.13; etc.

Numbering systems are useful for distinguishing main from subsidiary points:

In business the word 'competition' may denote:

1 A <u>state of affairs</u> that includes
   (a) increasing sales in competition with rivals
   (b) avoiding loss of customers to rivals
   (c) advantageous purchasing
2 A <u>process</u> that can take the form of
   (a) launching new, attractive products
   (b) sales promotions of existing products

(The underlining picks out the two major denotations of 'competition'.)

Exercise 2

Arrange and number the details in 1 and 2 below in note form, underlining two or three important words or phrases:

1 The American settlers had two methods of preserving their smoked hams. The first method was to sew linen cloths round the hams and then whitewash them all over with lime; the limed parcels were then washed four or five times and dried in the sun between washings. The second method was to put fine sifted wood ash at the bottom of a wooden chest, lay in the first ham, cover it with more ash, lay on the second ham, and then cover all with another layer of ash. Both methods preserved the hams perfectly.

2 In the sea, swimming just above the substratum, are fishes, opossum shrimps, cuttlefishes, and similar creatures, and crawling or walking on the substratum are starfishes, crabs, lobsters, and other animals; beneath its surface are burrowing worms, brittle-starfishes, heart-urchins, crabs, and other creatures.

Brevity

Abbreviations help to make notes concise. There are many well-known standard abbreviations, full lists of which are given at the back of the *Concise Oxford Dictionary* and *Chambers' Twentieth Century Dictionary*. You can also invent abbreviations of your own that suit your particular subject. Constantly recurring names may be referred to by their initials.

Be careful not to over-abbreviate. You will want notes that are comprehensible when you return to them at a later date. If you invent some special abbreviations for a particular set of notes, write a key to them on the first page of the notes.

Many of the standard Latin and English abbreviations that we have already looked at in Chapter 6 are useful for notes. Some of them are mentioned again in the list of abbreviations and symbols below:

b.	born	e.g.	for example
d.	died	i.e.	that is
m.	married	cp.	compare
ed.	edited by	c.	about (of time)
pub.	published by	p.	page
ch.	chapter	pp.	pages
fig., figs	figure, figures	para.	paragraph
vol., vols	volume, volumes	opp.	opposite
bk., bks	book, books	NB	(nota bene) note well
pt., pts	part, parts		

C^{18}, C^{19}	eighteenth century, nineteenth century
$\therefore$	therefore
$\because$	because
?	perhaps
>	greater than
<	less than
=	equals
+	plus, and

Exercise 3

Rewrite the sentences below, shortening them by using abbreviations and condensing meanings where possible:

1 For an account of the state of science around 1798, see Sir Harold Hartley's *Humphrey Davy*, pages 1–8.
2 Figure 3 in part one should be compared with figures 8 and 9 in part two.
3 We should question whether nineteenth-century politics were as buoyantly optimistic as they are sometimes said to have been.
4 The Purple Emperor butterfly is larger than the White Admiral and the White Admiral is larger than the Comma.

Abbreviations are especially useful when taking notes quickly at a lecture. But their use does not guarantee that your notes will be good notes, for the aim is not to reproduce everything in shorthand. A vital skill is that of selecting important words and phrases so that the main points of a passage come to life at a glance when you re-read your notes at a later date. Taking very brief notes at a lecture by using the technique of picking out 'reminder' words, and then writing up your notes more fully afterwards, is a very effective way of learning new material. But if your first notes are very brief, don't allow too much time to pass before writing your fuller version of them.

In the example below I have picked out important words from the sentence at (a) to make one very short note at (b):

(a) One of the contributory factors to *Castlereagh's suicide*, according to popular *gossip* at the time, was an element of *mental instability* in his *family*.
(b) Castlereagh's suicide – gossip – mental instability in family?

Exercise 4

Underline important words and phrases in the sentences below and write very short notes from them, using abbreviations where suitable:

1 The first person known to have made a scientific study of the way yoghurt is made was a Russian biologist, Ilya Metchnikoff, at the beginning of this century, when he was working at the Lister Institute in Paris with Pasteur.

2 Theology described as 'revealed theology' was a body of doctrine based on God's revelation to man through Christ, Scriptures, and the Church; and it has to be compared with 'natural theology', which was knowledge of God held to be obtainable simply by reasoning about the natural universe.

3 Sir Arthur Conan Doyle, who was born in Edinburgh in 1859, is well known for his books about Sherlock Holmes. His influence on criminology was wide: the Chinese and Egyptian police used Conan Doyle's works as official training text books, and J. Edgar Hoover made no secret of the fact that the FBI adopted Conan Doyle's methods of detection.

4 T. S. Eliot has said that the primary channel of transmission of culture is the family. But, he points out, the family is not the only channel; culture may be transmitted by the life-style (as distinct from the book-learning) of universities, by communities of craftsmen, and by the traditions of organisations and societies.

Summarising is important if notes are to be concise; but it must be done carefully, so as not to distort meaning or emphasis. An idea, a meaning, or an argument, must be properly grasped before it can be accurately summarised. Read the short extract below, and decide which of the two brief summaries, (a) or (b), is better:

The reader who skims is like an observer on the look-out: he has a perspective; he keeps his eyes skinned; and he reacts with speed. Skimming is faster than fast reading, because the reader also uses the field of vision that lies outside his normal reading span.

(a) The skimmer is *an observer on the look-out*. Skimming is faster than fast reading ∴ reader uses wider-than-normal span.
(b) The skimmer
  (i) has a perspective
  (ii) keeps his eyes skinned
  (iii) reacts with speed
  (iv) uses wider-than-normal reading span

In my opinion (a) is a slightly better summary than (b), in spite of the orderliness of the latter. In (a) the quoted phrase 'observer on the look-out' neatly encapsulates the essence of skimming. Its second sentence explains how the broad coverage and great speed of skimming are achieved. The summary at (b) makes a tidy list of points, but it does not distinguish the more important from the less; nor does it pinpoint the essential 'look-out' characteristic of skimming in the way that (a) does.

Exercise 5

Write brief, accurate summaries of the passages below:

1 When lecturing, a point should first of all be stated in as concise a way as possible; in a short sentence, say, introducing a key word or phrase. The key word or phrase should then be displayed on the blackboard or screen as part of a developing scheme of such reminders. The point should then be re-stated in another way. The change of wording allows those who did not understand the first statement a second chance to take the point; and it reinforces the understanding of those who did grasp it the first time.

2 There really is no such thing as Art. There are only artists. Once these were men who took coloured earth and roughed out the forms of a bison on the wall of a cave; today they buy their paints, and design posters for the Underground; they did many things in between. There is no harm in calling all these activities art as long as we keep in mind that such a word may mean very different things in different times and places, and as long as we realise that Art with a capital A has no existence.

More techniques

Diagrams, tables, charts, and schematic layouts using connecting lines and arrows are sometimes extremely helpful for organising material chronologically, sorting facts and information, showing connexions or divisions between ideas, and revealing the larger structure or development of a topic. These sorts of techniques are particularly useful once you have accumulated quite a lot of notes on a topic and are reorganising or revising them. One excellent way of revising and testing your knowledge of a topic is to read through your notes, writing down major headings on a large schematic diagram as you do so; then, when you have read the notes, close your file and try filling in your diagram in a concise and orderly way. A biographical topic in its first schematic form, awaiting details, might look something like this:

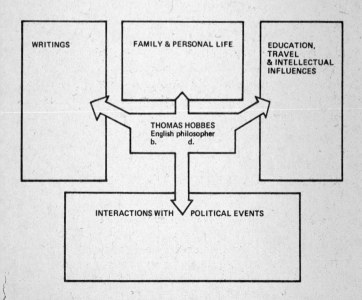

Connexions between detailed notes written in the panels may be indicated by coloured lines.

Schematic diagrams and layouts do not have to be of regular geometric shapes. Informal schemes often serve very well, especially for indicating relationships between categories or for adding subsidiary pockets of information after the main layout has been drawn:

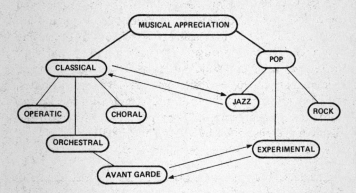

Schematic diagrams are, on the whole, more useful for amassing facts and recording processes or sequences than for setting out arguments or controversies. Some people find them a great help in memorising the main themes or concepts of a topic area.

Exercise 6
Make a schematic diagram to accommodate notes on the following:

Efficient study requires not one but several related skills that interact with or complement one another. The skill of reading selectively and with a definite purpose complements the skills of note-taking. The skill of writing clearly benefits essay work, report writing, and note-taking; while the skills of analysis and evaluation are useful for every aspect of study. And all of these skills, for their best use, must be exercised from the impetus of a steady motivation, compounded of the student's goals, interests, needs, and ambitions.

The ability to paraphrase is important not only for note-taking but also for the whole activity of learning; for if you can accurately express an idea in your own words then you have, in a sense, made it your own. In notes, good paraphrasing condenses meaning by eradicating the discursive words and reiterations that are an aid to first understanding but are unnecessary once an idea is fully understood. The rather wordy passage at (a) below is from an essay called 'Everyday Art', collected in *Short Essays on the Arts Not-fine*, written by L. F. Day in 1882. I have paraphrased it at (b):

(a) We cannot do without common sense, even though at times it be so common as not greatly to commend itself to us. Men who live by their art have as little right to despise the pecuniary considerations attaching to its connection with manufacture and commerce as to pander to what they believe to be vulgarity, or prostitute their art to money-getting. The profit that an artist derives from commerce puts him in a better position to carry out his own idea of what is best in art, and to insist upon a higher and still higher standard of excellence in the manufacture for which he designs.

(b) Common sense is indispensable, even though it is often disregarded. Artists have as little right to ignore the fact that art earns money as they have to abuse their art in order to make money. Profit from art enables the artist to insist on the best, both in his own design and its manufacture.

Exercise 7

Write brief paraphrases of the passages below:

1 Laymen sometimes use the word 'demand' to mean purchases or orders. In either case they are thinking of a single figure of, say,

packets per month or tons per year. The economist, on the other hand, uses 'demand' in a special sense to indicate the whole set of factors determining purchases or orders. For him, demand is thus a relationship between the things that determine purchases on the one hand, and the amount that people buy (or order) on the other.

2 A spadeful of soil may look a very simple innocuous substance. But it is, in fact, of such enormous complexity that it is doubtful if mankind will ever fully understand it. First of all, if it is good soil, it is filled with life. In every teaspoonful of soil there are millions of bacteria – bacteria of numerous species as well as algae, microscopic animals, the mycelium of fungi, and viruses.

An efficient way of amassing factual information in note form is with a card-index system. Suppose you wanted to write about Shakespeare's allusions to herbs in his plays. Then you could read through the plays and whenever you found mention of a herb, note down the play, act, scene, and lines in which the allusion occurs, having headed your card with the name of the herb:

ROSEMARY
Hamlet, Act IV, Scene 5, l. 158

Depending on the exact purpose of your enquiry you may wish also to note who spoke the lines, or to quote the phrase that mentions the herb; or you may wish to classify the context of the allusion, as, for instance, 'love-scene', or 'medicinal', or 'magical'. The great advantage of cards for these sorts of notes is that they can be shuffled and sorted in ways that give you fresh perspectives on your enquiry. For instance, if all the cards that cite comedies as sources of herbal allusions are placed together and their information considered, then something interesting may come to light; and similarly with the cards that note women as the speakers of the lines, or the context as 'medicinal', and so on.

Exercise 8

Suppose you were investigating the significance of the colour blue in Florentine Renaissance paintings from 1400 to 1450 containing the figure of the Virgin Mary, and wanted to collect your notes in a card-index system. Say what kind of subject-heading you would give your cards (that is, the equivalent of the individual herb names I suggested in the Shakespeare example above), and list four sub-headings for the categories of the information to be noted on each card.

Notes of arguments

Condensing an argument into note form can be difficult work. But the struggle is usually worth while: sorting out just what is being asserted and what is being said to support the assertion often reveals the strengths and weaknesses of the argument.

First, try to pick out the main assertion (called the *conclusion*) of the argument. It often occurs at the beginning, although not always. If it is not at the beginning, look out for words such as *thus*, *hence*, *therefore*, *it follows*; for they often indicate that a conclusion is about to be stated. When you have identified the conclusion, sort out the individual points that support it. These are the premises of the argument.

Layout is important for showing the structure of an argument. Below is an argument, set out in note form, in which I have placed the conclusion last:

Thousands die each year from illnesses caused by smoking
Many smokers deeply regret smoking
Much misery is caused by smoking
∴ Smoking should be banned.

In that layout I have used a fresh line to state each premise of the argument, and the ∴ (therefore) sign to mark the statement that is the conclusion of the argument.

You may prefer to put a conclusion first:

Smoking should not be banned
∵ (because)
A ban infringes personal liberty
We do not ban other dangerous habits and activities (e.g. drinking, contact sports).

At (a) below there is an argument about free will in which I have italicised the conclusion. At (b) I have put the argument into note form.

(a) The universe is a physical universe and works in accordance with deterministic laws that govern the movements of matter. *Human beings cannot have free will.* They are parts of the physical universe and are governed by the same deterministic laws as govern the movements of all matter.

(b) The universe is physical and governed by deterministic laws. Human beings are also physical and so governed by the same laws.
∴ Human beings cannot have free will.

Exercise 9

Set out in note form the arguments in the passages below. State each conclusion at the *end* of the argument, using the ∴ sign:

1 Our coal, thousands of people were saying, is the real basis of our national greatness; if our coal runs short, there is an end of the greatness of England.

2 Some mentally ill people may harm or kill other people. They should therefore be compulsorily confined to hospital. These sorts of people are also likely to harm or kill themselves.

When it is difficult to pick out an argument in a passage, first try asking the question: What is being asserted? The assertion may be in the form of a recommendation or a piece of advice, or it may be a rejection or a denial of something. Quite often an assertion that is in fact the conclusion of the argument is made at the beginning of the argument, and is followed by the points that support it. When you have found the assertion, underline it and then ask: What is being said to support it? In the passage at (a) below, the assertion that is the conclusion of the argument is made in the first sentence. At (b) I have set out the argument as briefly as possible:

(a) In moral matters it is unwise to ignore moral beliefs and to rely instead on intuitive responses. For one thing, intuitive responses may have little moral content: they may be determined by self-interest, by guilt or fear, or by conditioned attitudes acquired in childhood and never questioned or reviewed. It may even be the case that no single, clear, intuitive response occurs.

(b) Intuitive responses to moral problems may:
  (1) have little moral content;
  (2) be determined by self-interest, guilt, or fear;
  (3) be the result of unquestioned, conditioned attitudes;
  (4) be confused and unclear.
  ∴ In moral matters it is unwise to ignore general moral beliefs and to rely instead on intuitive responses.

Exercise 10

Identify the assertions that are the conclusions of the arguments in the following passages and put the arguments into brief note form:

1 If school pupils wear a uniform, then differences between their financial and social backgrounds are less apparent than if they wear no uniform. All schools should have some sort of uniform. It does away with problems of deciding what clothing to forbid and what to allow; it makes life simpler, and probably less expensive, for parents; and it engenders a spirit of community in the school itself.

2 Beautiful art can only be produced by people who have beautiful

137

things about them, and leisure to look at them; and unless you provide some elements of beauty for your workmen to be surrounded by, you will find that no elements of beauty can be invented by them.

Taking relevant notes

Quite often, you need to take notes for specific purposes; perhaps to gather information for a particular essay question that concentrates on a single aspect of a topic, a work, or a life. This will probably mean consulting a range of books, texts, and articles, using indexes and chapter headings to help you locate relevant passages, and employing a whole range of techniques to produce concise and accurate notes that bear directly on the question you have to answer. I shall use the whole of the remainder of this section for a single exercise on this kind of task.

Exercise 11

Using the sources quoted below, make notes relevant to answering the question: 'What was innovatory about Thomas Hobbes's political philosophy?' Remember to cite each source at the head of the notes you take from it:

1 ... Hobbes thought of his system of politics as a science. He was sure that politics could be made a science. He believed that he had done it, and that he was the first to have done it. His claims were bold. He wrote of 'the infallible rules and true science of equity and justice', of the duties of rulers and subjects as 'a science ... built upon sure and clear principles ...' And it was not just his claims that were bold, his science was too: as we shall see, he had truly caught the spirit of the new science that was transforming men's understanding of the natural world.

        C. B. Macpherson, Introduction to *Leviathan*, p. 10

2 Thomas Hobbes would have liked to live in safety in a well-run and stable society, reasoning for the benefit of mankind about

matters that interested him deeply. Finding himself instead in the midst of civil strife he felt compelled to seek a solution to the troubles that surrounded him. In *Leviathan*, published in England in 1651, he analysed human nature and civil society and propounded a form of government which he maintained would ensure peace and stability. Hobbes's greatness rests not so much on his prescription for securing peace as on the method by which he reached and justified that prescription; for he adventurously adopted the new scheme of concepts that was being developed in the physical sciences of the day and extended its use by applying it to human nature and civil society as well as to the material universe. He was the first to attempt a systematic account of matter, man and society that drew those subjects together within the scope of one method. He aimed at a complete and incontestable knowledge that would enable man to design a form of government that took account of the most elemental characteristics of human nature as well as the aspirations of human reason. It was through his method that he sought conclusions that were incontestable . . .

It was geometry that furnished Hobbes with a method. Its appeal lay in the incontrovertibility of its conclusions. Geometrical reasoning proceeds from a 'given', a basic premise or set of premises, and moves by step to conclusions which must follow from the premises and which cannot be otherwise. This is the deductive method. Hobbes's idea was to deduce a set of conclusions about the conduct of human affairs from a set of premises about human nature. This would result in what he called 'a science of politics'. By 'science' Hobbes meant, in common with other seventeenth century thinkers, a body of knowledge arrived at by means of deductive reasoning, rather than what is nowadays meant by the word.

Open University correspondence unit

3 . . . Hobbes does not mean that geometry itself can be used in studying human behaviour. He means that the method of reasoning used by the geometer is the proper scientific method, to be applied to any study that aims at being scientific.

D. D. Raphael, *Hobbes*, p. 20

4 Thomas Hobbes
The day of his birth was April the fifth, Anno Domini 1588, on

a Fryday morning, which that yeare was Good Fryday. His mother fell in labour with him upon the fright of the Invasion of the Spaniards ...

At fower yeer old Mr Thomas Hobbes (Philosopher) went to Schoole in Westport Church till 8 – then the church was painted. At 8 he could read well and number a matter of 4 or 5 figures. After, he went to Malmesbury to Parson Evans ...

At fourtenn years of age, he went away a good Schoole-scholar to Magdalen-hall in Oxford ...

He was 40 years old before he looked on geometry; which happened accidently. Being in a Gentleman's Library, Euclid's Elements lay open, and 'twas the 47 El. libri I. He read the proposition. *By G—*, sayd he, (he would now and then sweare an emphaticall Oath by way of emphasis) *this is impossible!* So he reads the Demonstration of it, which referred him back to such a Proposition; which proposition he read. That referred him back to another, which he also read ... This made him in love with Geometry.

John Aubrey, 'Thomas Hobbes', *Aubrey's Brief Lives*,
pp. 305, 307, 309

5 He (Hobbes) was right in making claims for the originality of his civil philosophy; for he attempted to establish political science and psychology as objective studies, untrammelled by theological assumptions or moral convictions ... He tried to explain the behaviour of men in the *same sort of way* as he explained the motion of bodies. This was a comparatively novel undertaking at that time.

R. S. Peters, *Hobbes*, p. 74

Revision exercises

Exercise 12
Make short notes from the following, using abbreviations and symbols:

1 At the beginning of the year 1845 the state of Ireland was, as it had been for nearly seven hundred years, a source of grave anxiety to England. Ireland had first been invaded in 1169; it was

now 1845, yet she had been neither assimilated nor subdued.

2 Joseph Conrad's important novel, *Chance*, was first published in 1913 by Methuen.

3 We are now fairly certain that there is some form of vegetation on Mars; the seasonal colour changes, coupled with recent spectroscopic evidence, give this a high degree of probability.

4 In the group of wind instruments called recorders, the bass recorder is larger than the tenor, the tenor larger than the alto, the alto larger than the treble. Smallest of them all is the high-pitched sopranino.

Exercise 13

Underline important words and phrases in the following sentences and make very short notes from them:

1 The main field of Lavoisier's scientific work between 1778 and 1783 was his collaboration with Laplace in the study of thermo-chemistry. Together they invented the ice calorimeter, by which they determined heats of reaction and combustion.

2 Research begins with a question, putting into words a specific curiosity. The next step is to make a guess at the answer, or to 'formulate a hypothesis'.

3 Defoe was our first great novelist because he was our first great journalist, and he was our first great journalist because he was born, not into literature, but into life.

4 Each of us possesses an active and a passive vocabulary. Our active vocabularies are made up of the words we habitually use in talking and writing. Our passive vocabularies are made up of words we understand but do not generally use.

Exercise 14

Write a paraphrase of the following:

To understand the nature and quantity of Government proper for man, it is necessary to attend to his character. As nature created him for social life, she fitted him for the station she intended. In all cases she made his natural wants greater than his individual powers.

No one man is capable, without the aid of society, of supplying his own wants; and those wants, acting upon every individual, impel the whole of them into society, as naturally as gravitation acts to a centre.

Thomas Paine, *The Rights of Man*, p. 157

Exercise 15
Put the argument of the passage below into note form:

The human animal requires a spatial territory in which to live that possesses unique features, surprises, visual oddities, landmarks, and architectural idiosyncrasies ... A neatly symmetrical, geometric pattern may be useful for holding up a roof, or for facilitating the prefabrication of mass-produced housing-units, but when such patterning is applied at the landscape level, it is going against the nature of the human animal. Why else is it fun to wander down a twisting country lane? Why else do children prefer to play on rubbish dumps or in derelict buildings, rather than on their immaculate, sterile, geometrically-arranged playgrounds?

Desmond Morris, *The Human Zoo*, p. 211

Exercise 16
Make brief notes from the passage below on the life of Thomas Paine:

Thomas Paine was born in Thetford in 1737, the son of a Quaker Staymaker. After several years at sea, in the excise, and at staymaking, Paine went to America in 1774 at the age of thirty-seven and edited the *Pennsylvania Magazine*. Two years later he published *Common Sense*, a tract in favour of republicanism ... *Common Sense* inspired the first moves towards the American Declaration of Independence of July 1776 (drafted by his friend Thomas Jefferson, the future president). Paine was appointed secretary of a commission sent out by the newly established Congress to treat with the Indians, and later secretary of the Congressional Committee on Foreign Affairs ... he returned to Europe in 1787 at the age of fifty. In England he associated with societies that were spreading ideas of liberty. It was almost inevitable that he should reply to Burke's *Reflections*, which he did in three months in Part I of *The Rights of Man*, published in March 1791 ...

Part II of *The Rights of Man* was strong meat, too strong for the government of the day, which indicted Paine for treason in May 1792, and on the same day issued a proclamation against 'seditious writings' ...

In 1802 he (Paine) sailed to America but found his popularity had evaporated. He died in New York in 1809 at the age of 72. His body was removed to England in 1819 by William Cobbett.

Arthur Seldon, Introduction to Thomas Paine, *The Rights of Man*,
pp. v, vi, xii, and xiii

8 Essay writing

This chapter concentrates on techniques for writing those essays which are part of course work and which are planned and prepared with the help of notes and text books. It presents a step-by-step method for the work.

Writing examination essays and answers requires a somewhat different approach which is discussed in Chapter 9. The discussion points out the differences between tackling routine essays and examination answers and shows how good practice in tackling the routine essay can benefit examination work.

Basic form

Writing an essay doesn't mean using long words and lofty phrases. Matthew Arnold's advice was, 'Have something to say and say it as clearly as you can'.

There is not one set form in which an essay should be written, yet an essay certainly requires a form or shape: it is not just a string of paragraphs that refer loosely to its question or title. The paragraphs of an essay must relate to each other and to the essay subject in ways that clearly exhibit a development of thought or argument that meets the demands of the question. (In general, I shall use the word 'question' to refer to the title, subject, topic, etc. of an essay.)

A basic form for an essay may nearly always be derived from the form of the essay question. For instance, 'Assess the arguments for and against the proposal "Let us abolish breakfast"' suggests a basic, three-part form:

- arguments for the proposal;
- arguments against it;
- assessments.

The basic form may be set out in a way that provides scope for its development:

'Let us abolish breakfast'

For	*Against*

Assessments

Basic form is not always easily derived from the essay question. For example, the instruction 'Critically discuss . . .' does not immediately suggest a basic form. But as soon as we think carefully about what it means to be 'critical' and to 'discuss', it becomes apparent that here again is a request for a weighing of fors and againsts. Usually it is short or one-word essay titles that do not suggest an obvious form; but with those sorts of titles the subject-matter itself sometimes gives guidance. A controversial subject such as 'Early Retirement' slips easily into the for-and-against form. Difficult concepts such as 'Anarchy' and 'Culture' invite close discussion of their meanings and the citing of examples and counter-examples. A question such as 'What is Art?' is not dealt with as easily as its simple directness may suggest. A bold opening answer or claim, followed by a discussion of objections to it, is one possible form. Alternatively, the essay might begin by denying the possibility of a neat answer, and then go on to build up a detailed discussion of the concept of art.

Exercise 1
Construct basic forms for each of the following essay questions, setting them out diagrammatically if you can:

1 Do we lead softer lives than our grandparents did?
2 Does scientific advance erode or strengthen religious belief?
3 Is pride much the same as vanity?

Answers for Chapter 8 are on pp. 215–23.

A basic form must be developed into an essay plan that can be given content. Most essay questions contain key words that assist this development; you probably became aware of some of them as you constructed basic forms for the essay questions above. Some key words are instructions such as 'Explain . . .' or 'Describe . . .' that make clear the sort of treatment that the essay topic requires. Some are concepts or ideas that you will need to explore or analyse in order to deal properly with the question. When you develop a basic form into an essay plan, key words can help you to choose sub-sections and content for your essay.

In the question below I have italicised what I think are the key words:

Critically discuss the view that '*genius* is ten per cent *inspiration*, ninety per cent *perspiration*'.

Comment
● 'Critically discuss . . .' – these are instruction words that tell us how to treat the topic.

- 'genius' – *the* important concept that must be explored in the essay.
- 'inspiration' – another important concept, closely linked to that of genius.
- 'perspiration' – in this context a metaphor for 'hard work', and an important element in the discussion.

Exercise 2

Underline the key words in the following essay questions:

1 What arguments are there against the contention that no one today can be regarded as well educated without a knowledge of general science?
2 Contrast and compare the benefits of city life with those of country life.
3 If you had to choose, which would you take: a contented life as a nonentity, or a turbulent life of fame? Give reasons for your choice.

The essay plan

A careful look at the key words that tell you what to do can greatly ease the task of developing a basic form into an essay plan. Questions often begin with words such as 'Discuss ...' or 'Explain ...', or phrases such as 'Account for ...' or 'Contrast and compare ...'. If you are clear about the particular approaches those terms require, you will be able to develop your essay plan quickly and confidently and deploy your material effectively.

Exercise 3

Briefly state the exact meaning of each of the essay instructions listed below. Use a dictionary to help you if necessary:

Discuss ...
Explain ...
Argue for ...
Analyse ...
Summarise ...
Evaluate ...
Define ...
Critically examine ...
Outline ...
Justify ...
Describe ...
Contrast and compare ...

There is not a lot of difference between some of the instruction terms above. 'Summarise' and 'Outline' have a lot in common, as do 'Justify ...' and 'Argue for ...', and also 'Critically examine ...' and 'Evaluate ...'. You have probably noticed already that many essay questions ask you, in one way or another, to give reasons or weigh evidence for or against particular assertions and opinions. Quick recognition of these requirements and an appreciation of how they differ from describing, outlining, and giving an account of are important for the exact tailoring of your essay to the demands of the question.

So far we have treated as more or less separate items the tasks of deriving a basic form and picking out key words. In practice they are scarcely separable, and a third task, that of expanding the basic form into an essay plan to which content can be given, is a logical development of the first two.

Below, I have amalgamated the three tasks to develop an essay plan from the basic form of the question on p. 145. I have italicised the key words:

Assess the *arguments for* and *against* the proposal, 'Let us abolish breakfast'.

'Let us abolish breakfast'

For abolition	Against abolition
Arguments about health and diet	⟶
Social and practical considerations	⟶
Other arguments (economic, light-hearted?)	⟶

Assessments

Obvious non-controversial judgements
More debatable and complex ones
Humorous point for ending?

Notice that what is required by way of content for the essay gradually begins to emerge as the basic form of the essay is developed into a plan by thinking carefully about the question.

Exercise 4

Make an outline plan for the following essay question, paying close attention to instruction words and any difficult concepts:

Discuss the claim that science and technology do more than the arts to make a society civilised.

Content for the plan

When you read through an essay question for the first time you may immediately find ideas about it crowding into your head, or you may feel you will have to do quite a lot of reading and thinking before you start writing. Preparatory reading will be discussed in the next section. In this section I shall assume that you already have some ideas and that the problem before us is that of incorporating them into the essay plan in an intelligible and orderly way. What is needed is a method of arranging ideas and points without having to write them out over and over again.

Below are instructions for a simple numbering method which saves a lot of rewriting and which is adaptable to almost any kind of essay plan. To illustrate the method I shall use the essay plan for the 'Let us abolish breakfast' question.

Read through the steps of the method:

- Have your essay plan before you. On a separate piece of paper, or below your plan if there is plenty of space, write the *broad* headings of your essay plan, e.g. 'For', 'Against'. Briefly jot down all your ideas for your essay, just as they occur to you, but placing them under the appropriate broad headings so that you end up with two or three columns of points.
- Give numbers to the sub-sections of your essay plan.
- Return to your columns of points. *Using a pencil*, number your points according to the sections to which they relate: a 1 beside each point that relates to section 1, a 2 beside each point for section 2, and so on.
- Your points are now grouped by numbers. Order the points *within* the groups in the following way: 1.1, 1.2, 1.3; 2.1, 2.2, 2.3, etc. Using a pencil for all this means that you can erase or improve upon your first arrangements if you wish.

You should now be able to write your essay in an orderly way by referring to your numbered points and your essay plan.

Exercise 5

This exercise will probably take longer than any you have worked so far. Below is the essay plan for 'Assess the arguments for and against the proposal "Let us abolish breakfast"', and with it, under the broad headings of the plan, are columns of points and ideas for the essay. Using a pencil, number the points down the sides of the columns to allocate them to appropriate sections of the plan; then order the points within their groups:

'Let us abolish breakfast'

For	Against
1 Arguments about health and diet	
2 Social and practical considerations	
3 Other arguments (economic, light-hearted?)	

Assessments

4 Obvious, non-controversial judgements
  More debatable and complex ones
  Humorous point for ending?

Points for essay For abolition of breakfast	Against abolition of breakfast	Assessments
No washing-up in morning	General health bound to suffer	Abolition almost certainly bad for children, elderly, and 'physical' workers
General health better?	Bad for slimming because huge lunch needed	
Could get up later		Health/diet arguments against abolition are mostly strong ones
Would suit working parents	Loss of family occasion	
Time to get up properly	Bad for 'physical' workers	Might be good for *some* to rearrange whole eating pattern: 'brunch' at
Does away with family breakfast squabbles	Bad for grocers	
	No incentive to get up	

continued on p. 152

For abolition of breakfast	Against abolition of breakfast	Assessments
Aid to slimming	Bad for children and elderly	eleven a.m., early evening meal
	Bad for cereal growers and manu-facturers	Abolition might be good for some adults and overweights whose lifestyle it suited
	Bad for everyone in cold weather	

Six recommendations for writing an essay

In the previous three sections we plunged straight into the business of looking at essay questions and making plans for their answers. In this section we shall pause to review the whole process of preparing to write an essay.

Exercise 6

Below are six recommendations for preparing an essay. Number or list them in the order in which you think they should be carried out:

( ) Assemble the books and notes you will need to use when writing the essay.

( ) Develop an outline plan that will deal systematically with the question.

( ) Read the question carefully to see exactly what it means and what it requires you to do. Devise a basic form for the essay, noting key words in the question.

( ) Jot down the main points that you think should be included in the essay and fit them into the essay plan.

( ) Refer back to the question to check that you are actually doing what it asks of you.

( ) Write a short opening paragraph to the essay and/or a short paragraph embodying your main idea, conclusion, argument, or claim.

Your ordering of the recommendations may be different from mine but I doubt whether it is *very* different. Perhaps you put 'Jot down the main points' (4) before 'Assemble books and notes' (3). If so, you would not be hampering your preparatory work very much in my opinion; but it does seem to me that the business of assembling relevant books and notes, glancing at their titles and headings, and skimming passages here and there can help to generate ideas for the 'jotting down' stage on those occasions when the essay question itself does not stimulate a ready response. Thus, in practice, reading and jotting down may well be alternating activities, although how matters work out on a particular occasion depends largely on your state of knowledge when you start your preparatory work.

A word of warning: there is a danger in assembling a large number of books and notes around you. You may find yourself bogged down in reading and searching for material and so confused that you are unable to start writing the essay. Resist spending a disproportionate amount of time on this stage.

The sixth recommendation – to write a short paragraph – launches you into the essay itself. Writing one or two key paragraphs is vital. Even if you alter or reject them later on, they give you something to work on and with; something to which your other ideas and material may be related or from which they may be developed.

The recommendation to refer back is important not only at this stage of essay writing but at later stages also. It should be put into practice each time you finish a paragraph. It can save you from wasting time along false trails.

A last point about essay plans: when you are trying to develop a basic form into an essay plan, you will often see that there are several possible directions or patterns open to you. For instance, if you are putting forward 'fors' and 'againsts' you will have to decide whether to present all the points 'for' together and then present all the points 'against' together, or to alternate them. You will also have to decide whether to make your assessments or evaluations at stages throughout the essay or to present them together at the end. Once again, do not linger unduly over making decisions. Settle for what looks like the best procedure for your subject and once you have chosen a pattern of presentation keep to it throughout the essay.

Exercise 7

In the next section we shall turn attention to essay beginnings and endings and to the structure of paragraphs. As a preliminary, read the essay opening below and ask yourself if it is a good beginning. Write down one or two reasons for your judgement and any suggestions you may have for altering the opening.

The origins of the Italian Renaissance
I shall commence this essay by saying what I think are the most important and salient features of the Italian Renaissance. I hasten to add that what I write can only be my own subjective view, based on the very limited reading which is all I have time for, and so some of the emphases and points made in this essay may seem rather offbeat.

It is not at all easy to say when or how the Italian Renaissance began. What seems to be certain is that it was closely connected with the revival of classical learning.

Beginnings, endings, and paragraphs

Essays have to have beginnings and endings but they don't have to have formal 'introductory' and 'concluding' paragraphs. However, although an essay need not have a formal introduction, its opening paragraph is often introductory in the sense that it makes statements or raises issues that indicate the scope and pattern of the essay.

What do you think of the following passage as an opening for an essay on the question 'What are the essential characteristics of dramatic tragedy'?

Tragedy is essentially an imitation not of persons but of action and life, of happiness and misery. All human happiness or misery takes the form of action; the end aimed at is a certain kind of activity, not a quality. Character gives us qualities, but it is in our actions – what we do – that we are happy or the reverse.

Aristotle, The Art of Poetry, ch. 6

There is a lot of meaning, as well as the framework for a whole essay, in those three sentences. The first sentence confronts the essay question head-on with a definition that offers a broad analysis of dramatic tragedy. The second sentence singles out for emphasis one element of the definition: action. The third sentence reinforces the importance of this element. Each statement is a firm assertion that will need further analysis, discussion, and, above all, justification in the essay's development. Together, the statements provide a strong, concise opening that also introduces what is to follow. There is no superfluous preamble.

Exercise 8

Below are three openings for an essay, 'What is to be understood by the term "Culture"?' Place them in order of preference, briefly giving reasons for your choice:

Opening one
The term 'culture' has different associations according to whether we have in mind the development of an individual, or a group or class, or of a whole society.

Opening two
Civilisation in all its diversity now has a grip on practically every

region of the earth, so that all societies have music, art and literature woven into their ways of life.

Opening three
Somebody once said that when he heard the word 'culture' he reached for his gun. It might therefore be useful to start this enquiry by asking what it is about the word 'culture' that prompted such a reaction.

It isn't possible to pinpoint exactly what makes a satisfactory ending to an essay, because the effectiveness of an ending is largely dependent on what has gone before. Sometimes it is enough to make a strong, conclusive point that clinches your main argument. Sometimes a concise summary of main issues rounds off the essay effectively. Here is the last paragraph of A. J. P. Taylor's sizeable book *The Origins of the Second World War*. In a few plain sentences he manages to remind us of the crucial issues of his subject:

The British people resolved to defy Hitler, though they lacked the strength to undo his work. He himself came to their aid. His success depended on the isolation of Europe from the rest of the world. He gratuitously destroyed the source of this success. In 1941 he attacked Soviet Russia and declared war on the United States, two World Powers who asked only to be left alone. In this way a real world war began. We still live in its shadow. The war which broke out in 1939 has become a matter of historical curiosity.

Much of the merit of good beginnings and endings, and indeed of middles as well, derives from the structure of the paragraphs in which they are presented. Paragraphs show divisions of thought. A single paragraph, whether it is long or short, is a unity in that it contains one main idea which it develops, or a set of related thoughts. A new paragraph marks a shift or extension of ideas. Within an essay there must be strong connexions from paragraph to paragraph even though each paragraph is a coherent unity in itself.

Exercise 9

Comment critically on each of the following, paying particular attention to paragraph structure:

1 *Education in Britain today*

In Britain, a good education is supposed to be available to everyone. Unfortunately, the rich secure for themselves special educational advantages which, in one way or another, facilitate the perpetuation of their privileges and power. Wealth has always been able to buy authority and influence, and it is almost as difficult now as it has ever been for a poor man or woman to gain eminence and power. There is no real equality in this allegedly democratic nation.

2 *The good writer*

The writer I like has paragraphs varied in length, development, and organisation. He lets me know where he is going, moves quickly through simple material, and explains and illustrates more difficult points. His paragraphs are carefully connected, and when there is a marked change in thought, there are enough indications to help me follow the shift. He does not repeat unnecessarily or digress; instead, he covers his subject thoroughly and briefly. While I am still interested, he completes his work in a satisfactory final paragraph and leaves me wishing that there were more writers like him.

H. J. Tichy, *Effective Writing*, p. 259

3 *The rise of technology*

Man has always employed technology: he is a tool-making animal. The use of water, wind and fire goes back to the earliest days of civilisation as do techniques for measuring and building.

Work with levers is of similar early origin. Primitive crafts and trades have developed slowly over many centuries. Yet it was not until the nineteenth century that the great burgeoning of technology that transformed the world in a few decades took place. Only then was a systematic approach made to technological problems.

4 *The uses of television*

There is no doubt that television can be a powerful force in education, not only in that it can be used as a teaching aid at all levels in schools and colleges, but also in the wider sense that it can act as a disseminator of ideas, attitudes and points of view. It can offer new perspectives to vast audiences. In the USA, television is available all day and all night, and has only one channel that is without 'commercials'. Many American families keep their TV set – or sets – switched on for all their waking hours.

Referring back; revision exercises

The recommendation to refer back to the question is best carried out by asking: Does what I have written help to answer the question?

Exercise 10

Read through each passage below, checking back to its title for relevance and appropriateness to it. Mark any phrases, sentences, etc. that do not relate directly to what is at issue. Remember to make sure you understand exactly what each essay question means, by picking out and thinking about its key words:

1 'Unhappiness is best defined as the difference between our talents and our expectations. Is it?'

Unhappiness is a state that no one would wish to be in for any length of time. It is scarcely possible to imagine a human life without some periods of unhappiness. Unhappiness may arise from an individual's own temperament and attitudes, from unfortunate life circumstances, from relationships with other people, or from sudden tragedy or disaster.

2 'Is astrology a science?'

It would be interesting, and probably revealing, to know just what proportion of British adults turn eagerly and regularly to the 'What the Stars Foretell' sections of the weekly magazines.

One suspects that it is done by many who would never confess to such an interest. But there is no doubt that astrology exercises a very strong fascination over the minds of even highly rational and well-educated persons, although most of them refuse to admit it.

If astrology were a science, would these people be so ashamed of their interest? Would not astrology rate much as weather-forecasting does, that is, as an inexact science that is of open and legitimate concern to all of us?

The last part of this section consists of revision exercises that range over the whole chapter.

Exercise 11
If you were asked to give just *one* piece of advice on essay-writing, what would it be?

Exercise 12
Read the following:

Whether it is long or short, a paragraph develops one main idea. The central idea may be stated in one sentence – the topic sentence. This may appear anywhere in the paragraph. Often it opens or closes a paragraph, but sometimes the topic sentence is so obvious that it is not expressed.

H. J. Tichy, *Effective Writing*, p. 263

Which is 'the topic sentence' in that paragraph?

Exercise 13
Write a short opening paragraph for the essay 'Assess the arguments for and against the proposal "Let us abolish breakfast"'. If you wish, relate your opening to the material and plan on p. 151.

Exercise 14

Construct a basic form for the following essay title:

State and analyse what it is you like so much about one of your favourite novels.

9 A note on writing examination answers

The examination essay

There are two main differences between writing a routine course essay and writing an essay in an examination. The first difference is between the length of planning time available for each kind of essay. The second is between resources: for a routine essay, books and notes are available; for most examination essays you have only your memory and intelligence to rely on. Good habits in tackling routine essays can benefit your examination writing. In the examination it is essential to read the question carefully, to note its key words, and to construct a basic form. If you are practised in those techniques you should be able to plan your essay, organise its main points, and start writing your answer in less than five minutes. If you have trained yourself not to indulge in lengthy 'introductions', you will go straight to the heart of the question and deal with it directly and cogently. If you have not been in the habit of writing elaborate winding-up paragraphs, you will not waste precious examination time on them. If you have developed a skill in jotting down points and ordering them by numbers, then you will find you have plenty to say and can arrange it coherently.

Of course, to write a good examination answer you must know your subject as well as you possibly can. You must have done your reading, note-taking, learning, and thinking. But even all that is not enough. In an examination you have to write clearly in a limited time, and the only way to do that well is *to practise doing it*. When you have worked on a particular topic for a while and are beginning to feel you have some grasp of it, find one or two appropriate questions – or invent them – and then plan and write answers to them under examination conditions.

Referring back to the essay question to check that what you are writing answers it, is just as important in an examination as in routine essay-writing. If you have established this as a habit it is very likely that you will find yourself doing it quite naturally in the examination.

Tackling an examination paper

- Before you go into the examination room, make sure you know how long the examination lasts, how many questions you are required to answer in the time, and whether time is to be allocated equally to the questions. Calculate how much time you will be able to give to each question.
- When the examination begins, read carefully the instructions on the paper that tell you which questions, if any, are compulsory, how many you must or may answer from each section, and so on. *Put a tick beside any compulsory questions.*
- Read right through the paper (or through all the sections that concern you). Put a mark beside any questions you can answer well or adequately. If there are one or two questions you are certain you will answer, put ticks beside them. At this stage it does not matter if you cannot settle *all* the questions you are going to answer.
- Pick out the best question for you, and tackle it. Keep an eye on the time. Try to finish a little before the question's share of time is up (you should be able to, if you are well prepared). Read through your answer to check

punctuation, spelling, etc. Resist any temptation to make large alterations unless you detect a real 'howler'. If there is anything you feel you want to add, put a note in the rough margin or on your rough paper. There may be time to write it in later. Leave space for what you wish to add.

- Tackle any compulsory questions next. Perhaps you prefer to *start* with compulsory questions in order to get them out of the way, but it is probably marginally better to begin with your best question (and of course, your best question may be one of the compulsory ones) so that you can get off to a good start.

- Check that you are complying with the instructions about choice of questions. If you have done all you are allowed to do in a particular block, put a line through the block so that you don't waste time re-reading questions you are not allowed to answer. Choose your next question from those you have ticked or marked and tackle it. Keep an eye on the time. Continue to work through the paper in this way.

- You may have difficulty in finding a last question you are able to answer. If so, quickly re-read the questions you did not mark the first time round: you may find one that will suit you after all. Don't waste a lot of time hovering between two or three equally difficult possibilities. Settle for one and do all you can with it. If you run completely out of steam, return to your earlier answers to make any additions you noted in rough. In any case, try to leave time to read through your whole paper in order to make minor corrections.

- If you do spend too much time on your first questions so that you find yourself with only five or ten minutes left to deal with the last one, write your answer to the last question in note form, outlining as much as possible of the content and development of a full answer.

Bibliography

The Concise Oxford Dictionary (Clarendon Press, Oxford)

Further reading

From the many books on usage and style I have chosen those
listed below to represent a range of interests in the subject.

Sir Ernest Gowers, *The Complete Plain Words* (Penguin Books,
1973)
This is a lively and entertaining book, originally
produced for civil servants to help them write in a clear,
jargon-free way, but of interest to anyone trying to achieve a
lucid style.

G. V. Carey, *Mind the Stop* (Penguin Books, 1977)
A small paperback which deals straightforwardly with the
standard conventions of punctuation; it is full of interesting
examples and sound advice.

B. A. Phythian, *A Concise Dictionary of Correct English*
(Hodder and Stoughton, 1979)
The entries explaining grammatical terms are particularly good
because they are detailed without being overwhelmingly so.
I know of no better *brief* handbook of correct usage.

H. W. Fowler, *Modern English Usage* (Oxford University
Press, 1978)

'Fowler's' was first published in 1926 and has become a classic, retaining relevance and usefulness by means of regular updating. It may be consulted for points of grammar, meanings of words, idioms, usage, and style.

A. S. Maney and R. L. Smallwood, eds, *MHRA Style Book* (MHRA, 1978)
The style book produced by the Modern Humanities Research Association gives precise and detailed guidance on the formal presentation of dissertations, papers, and all academic writing intended for publication. It includes guidance on proof correcting and a glossary of technical terms helpful to authors and editors.

George Orwell, 'Politics and the English Language', in *Shooting an Elephant and Other Essays* (Secker and Warburg, 1950)
Orwell's essay discusses metaphor, pretentious language, inflated style, and meaningless and misused words. His own style is a model of clarity and vigour.

Leonard Michaels and Christopher Ricks, eds, *The State of the Language* (University of California Press, 1980)
This book is a collection of essays about the very wide range of ways in which we use the language, looking at those ways as a record of how we inhabit and create our world.

Works cited

Aubrey, John, 'Thomas Hobbes', *Aubrey's Brief Lives* (Penguin Books, 1976)

Fowler, H. W., *Modern English Usage*, ed. Sir Ernest Gowers (Clarendon Press, 1978)

Holroyd, Michael, *Lytton Strachey* (Penguin Books, 1971)

Macpherson, C. B., Introduction to *Leviathan* (Penguin Books, 1977)

MacRae, Donald G., *Weber* (Fontana, 1974)

Michaels, L. and Ricks, C., eds, *The State of the Language* (University of California Press, 1980)

Morris, Desmond, *The Human Zoo* (Corgi Books, 1971)

Paine, Thomas, *The Rights of Man* (Everyman Paperbacks, 1969)

Peters, R. S., *Hobbes* (Penguin Books, 1967)

Powell, Anthony, *The Acceptance World* (Fontana, 1977)

Raphael, D. D., *Hobbes* (Allen and Unwin, 1977)

Seldon, Arthur, Introduction to *The Rights of Man* (Everyman, 1969)

Taylor, A. J. P., *The Origins of the Second World War* (Penguin Books, 1964)

Tichy, H. J., *Effective Writing* (New York: Wiley and Sons, 1966)

part three:
Answers to Exercises

1 Spot the mistakes

1

She was definately finding it difficult to keep up with the others.

fault Spelling.
correction definitely

2

The locomotive has it's own reserve power supply.

fault Punctuation: unnecessary apostrophe (*it's* is a shortening of 'it is').
correction its

3

When the obsession with deafening rock music is over.

fault Grammar: not a sentence.
correction e.g. I shall be glad when the obsession with deafening rock music is over.

4

The investment yielded an annual income of five hundred pounds a year.

fault Grammar: duplication of meaning.
correction The investment yielded an income of five hundred pounds a year.

5

We have been cognisant of the nature of this problem over a period of the order of a decade.

fault Wordy.
correction We have known about this problem for the past ten years.

6

I have now discussed the proposal for restocking all the deep freezers with my colleagues.

fault　　　Grammar: meaning confused by incorrect placing of words.

correction I have now discussed with my colleagues the proposal for restocking all the deep freezers.

7

The committee has not announced their decision yet.

fault　　　Grammar: singular followed by a plural.
correction The committee has not announced its decision yet.

　　　　Or: The committee·have not announced their decision yet.

8

It is esential to spell correctly.

fault　　　Spelling.
correction essential

9

The president of the society, acting on medical advice, has resigned his office and we have no alternative but to accept it .

fault　　　Grammar: meaning wrong ('it' refers to 'his office').
correction The president of the society, acting on medical advice, has offered his resignation, and we have no alternative but to accept it.

10

The owner of a piece of equipment, which does not comply with these regulations, is liable to a fine or imprisonment.

fault　　　Punctuation: unnecessary commas.
correction The owner of a piece of equipment which does not comply with these regulations is liable to a fine or imprisonment.

11

Add distilled water until there is five cubic centimetres of liquid in the test tube.

fault　　　Grammar: there is a singular where there should be a plural.

correction Add distilled water until there are five cubic centimetres of liquid in the test tube.

12

His illness can only be alleviated by drugs.

fault Grammar: meaning unclear because of placing of 'only'.
correction Only drugs can alleviate his illness.
Or: Drugs can only alleviate (but not cure) his illness.

13

The cause of the hold-up on the production-line was due to a fault in the conveyor-belt.

fault Grammar: duplication of meaning.
correction The cause of the hold-up on the production-line was a fault in the conveyor-belt.
Or: The hold-up on the production-line was due to a fault in the conveyor-belt.

14

The seminar ended by an open discussion.

fault Grammar: wrong word.
correction The seminar ended with an open discussion.

15

The drug produced unpleasant side-effects in a percentage of cases.

fault Meaningless use of 'percentage'.
correction The drug produced unpleasant side-effects in a (large? small?) percentage of cases.

16

There have been two magnificent victories for the British teams today, and they have won both of them.

fault Unnecessary duplication.
correction There have been two magnificent victories for the British teams today.

17

Many birds are now protected species, i.e. the osprey, the bittern, the golden eagle, the buzzard.

fault   Wrong use of i.e. (Latin *id est* = 'that is').

correction   Many birds are now protected species, e.g. the osprey, the bittern, the golden eagle, the buzzard. (Latin *exempli gratia* = 'for example')

18

He complained about the teaching, and then said he was completely disinterested in the subject anyway.

fault   Wrong use of 'disinterested'.

correction   He complained about the teaching, and then said he was completely uninterested in the subject anyway.

19

He literally made mincemeat of his opponent.

fault   Wrong use of 'literally' (one hopes).

correction   He made mincemeat of his opponent.

20

Before they arrived at the meeting they had already prepared their replies in advance.

fault   A triplication of meaning.

correction   They had prepared their replies before arriving at the meeting.

2 Spelling

Improve your spelling

Exercise 1

accommodate	deteriorate
vaccinate	February
committed	inoculate
particularly	parallel

arctic	access
contemporary	separate
miscellaneous	veterinary
recurrence	recognise

Note that *recognise* may be spelt with either an *s* or a *z*.

Exercise 2
1 'facination' should be *fascination*
2 'changable' should be *changeable*
3 'disatisfied' should be *dissatisfied*
  'penicillen' should be *penicillin*
4 'vallies' should be *valleys*
  'volcanos' should be *volcanoes*
5 'stationery' should be *stationary*
  'procede' should be *proceed*
  'manouevre' should be *manoeuvre*
  'inaudable' should be *inaudible*
6 'noticably' should be *noticeably*
  'transcendant' should be *transcendent*
  'contempory' should be *contemporary*

Exercise 3
1 veterinary, 2 February, 3 parallel, 4 deteriorate, 5 vaccination, inoculation, 6 particularly, arctic, 7 contemporary, recognise

Two spelling rules

Exercise 4
1 receive, 2 shield, 3 ceiling, 4 wield, 5 perceiving, 6 relief, 7 yields, 8 retrieve, 9 inconceivable, 10 conceited

Exercise 5
1 advertising, 2 recognising, 3 encouragement, 4 exploration, 5 arranging, 6 competing, 7 devastating

Exercise 6
The passage on p. 24 contains twenty-three mistakes. In the version below, the corrected words are italicised:

One day in *February* last year, while *practising* my clarinet, I became victim of an unfortunate event. Without warning, the *ceiling* of my study fell, *devastating* the careful *arrangement* of my books, music, and personal *possessions* that I had completed only the day before.

Strangely enough, this event was the *fulfilment* of a *prophecy* made by my sister when she visited me earlier that week. She had pointed out some obvious signs of *deterioration* in the *ceiling's* plasterwork, had peered at the *occasional* white flake on the table surface, and noted other small omens of *imminent* collapse. At the time I *dismissed* all this as *exaggeration*, thinking she was perhaps a little envious of the *independent* and *successful* life I had begun to lead once I had *separated* myself from the rest of the family, and so had *seized* the first opportunity to *generate* a little anxiety in my life. But to be fair to her, she was *appalled* when she subsequently learned she had indeed been a *prophet* of doom. Little did she know, when she offered to help put things right, that she was to be one of the *principal* characters in the *fascinating* and frightening events that were to ensue.

Latin and Greek plurals; similar words

Exercise 7

Singulars
appendix, crisis, datum, criterion, phenomenon, erratum, index, bacterium, maximum, memorandum, medium, parenthesis, stimulus, stratum, formula

Meanings
appendix = an addition
crisis = a turning point
datum = a fact, or something known
criterion = a standard for judging
phenomenon = an unusual occurrence
erratum = an error

index = listed contents of a book
bacterium = a microscopic organism
maximum = the greatest size or quantity of something
memorandum = a reminder, or aid to memory
medium = an agency, means,

or instrument
parenthesis = a bracketed
word or words
stimulus = an incentive or spur

stratum = a layer or horizontal
level
formula = an abbreviated
prescription, recipe, or set
of rules

Exercise 8

1 phenomena, 2 appendices, 3 criterion, 4 memorandum, 5 data
datum, 6 crises, 7 errata, 8 bacterium

Exercise 9

The following are the correct words:

1 principle, 2 effect, 3 practice, 4 stationery, 5 prophecy, 6 device,
7 dependent, dependants, 8 advice, 9 complement

The apostrophe

Exercise 10

1 the tree's shade, 2 the ass's braying, 3 the princess's education,
4 the men's boots, 5 the house's damp course, 6 the duchesses'
robes, 7 Rosemary's books, 8 the students' careers, 9 the armies'
losses, 10 the women's discussions

Exercise 11

1 Ulysses' wanderings, 2 the gas's properties, 3 Mr Jones's room, 4
one year's imprisonment, 5 the hippopotamus' lair, *or* the hippopotamus's lair, *or* the lair of the hippopotamus, 6 the potato's skin

('Ulysses's would not be wrong, but it is very sibilant when
spoken.)

Exercise 12

1 √, 2 i's, t's, 3 Mark's (*Joneses* is the plural of *Jones*; it is not a
possessive), 4 √, 5 it's (it is), Michael's, secretary's, 6 Matthew's,
John's, 6 It's (it is), children's, 7 collector's, 8 years' 9 year's

Exercise 13

There are twenty-five mistakes in the passage on p. 31. In the version below, the corrections are italicised:

It *isn't* easy to say exactly what it was about *Henry's* life, in those golden days of the *1960s*, that made *one's* own seem so unpromising. Certain *differences* were plain. His *father's* job meant that Henry was always meeting MPs and famous men, not to mention their daughters. His *mother's* money *guaranteed* that he never had to do a *day's* work to support himself. The idea of keeping up with the *Joneses* meant nothing to Henry, for his *life's* ambition was of another sort. His *heart's* desires bore no *resemblances* to yours or mine, for he *already* possessed everything that we might long for only in a *dream's* insanity.

I *can't* deny that my life then had *its* own glamour. Certainly, at the time, I *didn't* complain of a lack of *excitement*. All the *Henrys* in the world could not diminish my joy in *Anne's* love. Yet I had a sense of *opportunities* missed; and above all, a sense of the *gods'* disapproval, casting *its* shadow on the path before me.

Exercise 14
appendices, crises, indices, phenomena, errata

Common pitfalls

Exercise 15

governor	perpetrator	radiator
oppressor	deserter	gardener
painter	fertiliser	angler
donor	transmitter	confectioner
computer	incinerator	consumer
stationer	eraser	propellor
decorator	promoter	manufacturer
abettor (or abetter)	protector	possessor
purveyor	conqueror	creditor
inventor	motor	prosecutor

Exercise 16
The correct spellings are:
sovereign, professor, Mediterranean, privilege, aggravate, embarrass, disappear, leisure, fulfilment, nuisance, battalion, appalling, skilful

Exercise 17
1 cupped, 2 clapping, 3 canning, 4 cooling, fanning, 5 cropped, 6 drooping

Exercise 18

journeys	buffaloes
kangaroos	chimneys
lorries	gnus
turkeys	torpedoes
commandos	portfolios
kimonos	trolleys
tomatoes	wharfs, wharves
wolves	cities
studios	pianos
sopranos	jockeys
igloos	flamingos
calves	potatoes

Note: a few words that end with *o* in the singular form their plurals with either an *s* or an *es*, e.g. *eskimo* becomes either eskimos or eskimoes, *grotto* becomes either grottos or grottoes.

Revision exercises

Exercise 19

deteriorate	exaggerate
recognise	successful
parallel	veterinary

Exercise 20
The correct spellings are:

separate	committee
miscellaneous	particularly
accommodate	changeable
volcanoes	occasionally
contemporary	inoculate
recurrence	receive
weird	possessions

Exercise 21
1 phenomena, 2 media, 3 strata, 4 formulae, 5 maximum, 6 parentheses

Exercise 22
The passage on p. 36 contains forty mistakes. In the version below the corrections are italicised:

My *sister's eyes* widened as she surveyed my crumbling *ceiling*. I waited *until* she had recovered herself. 'Your *prophecy* is *fulfilled*', I said. 'It *happened* last night.'

Alicia was visibly *affected*. She *seized* my hand, '*I'm* coming to help with this', she said. '*I've* a *committee* meeting this morning to discuss the *accommodation* for the *VIPs* who are arriving next week, but after that *I'm* free. Why *don't* you do your clarinet *practice* in the bedroom this morning? *I'll* be back by lunchtime.'

With the prospect of a concert in two *weeks'* time, I was glad to be *relieved* of the burden of clearing up alone. *Alicia's efficiency* was as remarkable as her beauty, and I knew she excelled as a painter and *decorator*. Once we had cleared the room and the *ceiling's* plaster had been renewed, restoration would *proceed* apace under her *management*.

As I shook the dust from my music before *taking* it to the bedroom, I heard a kind of *scraping* noise that seemed to be *coming* from above the exposed laths of the *ceiling*. Fearful of a *recurrence* of the *night's* event, I made for the door, *glancing* as I did so at the hole above.

It was a moment of *crisis*. Even now I can hear the unmanly *shriek* that escaped me as I dived into the hall, *slamming* the door behind me. For my swift glance had *perceived* a horror almost beyond my *mind's* belief: the slithering, sinuous, *plopping* descent, from between the exposed laths°of the ceiling, of a large, befanged and *appallingly* evil-looking snake.

Exercise 23
1 transmitter, 2 stationery, confectionery, miscellaneous, 3 purveyor, manufacturer, 4 inventor, propellor, 5 possessor, computer

Exercise 24
1 Mr Jones, 2 Theseus' *or* the heroic exploits of Theseus, 3 digging, potatoes, 4 city's, chimneys, roofs, 5 lorry's (the second 'lorries' is correct), 6 It's, 7 one's, 8 principal, advice

3 Punctuation

Full stops and capital letters

Exercise 1
1 A sentence; so a stop is needed.
2 This is not a sentence as it contains no finite verb.
3 This is not a sentence as it has no subject.
4 A sentence; so a stop is needed.
5 A sentence; so a stop is needed.

Exercise 2
1 We meet on the last Wednesday of each month, except in July and August. Last month we visited the National Gallery in London.
2 The Rôyal Mile is the name of a famous street in Edinburgh. Have you every been there?
3 We are planning an expedition to the Swiss Alps so that we can photograph the lovely alpine flowers.
4 What a surprise! Whoever thought of this marvellous idea?
5 She reads the Bible regularly, and knows a great deal about biblical characters.
6 Are they both members of the Ambridge Social Club?

Exercise 3

1 We shall have to book a flight from Gatwick Airport. Do you mind having to fly?
2 He applied for a job with the British Broadcasting Corporation.
3 Do you know the painting called 'Virgin of the Rocks' by Leonardo da Vinci?
4 All the new peers will assemble in the House of Lords today. What a spectacle that will be!

Exercise 4

1 Mr W. Smith lives in Blossom Drive, next door to the Rev. James Brown.*
2 Have you a copy of *An ABC of English Usage*?
3 PC Smith of the Devon Constabulary is to appear on TV.
4 Miss Jane Wilton has sent me a party invitation. I see that it has an RSVP note on it.

The comma

Exercise 5

1 Incorrect. There should be a comma after 'did' as well as the one already placed after 'came'.
2 Correct.
3 Incorrect. There should be no comma after 'lever'; but there should be one after 'and'.
4 Correct.

Exercise 6

1 Strange words, obscure allusions, references to abstract ideas here and there, do not make a poem an important one.
2 Freud thought that art was a substitute for power, honour, riches, and the love of women.
3 The Surrealists wanted to dive into the subconscious mind, the mind below the conscious surface, and dig up the images from there.

Revd is also an acceptable abbreviation of *Reverend*. It is incorrect, when using the title *Reverend* (in any form), to omit initials or Christian name.

4 During the First World War three poets died who, if they had survived, would surely have altered the prevailing standards of poetry.

5 This anthology of critical essays will, I hope, be of interest to all students of poetry.

Exercise 7

Though his rowdy spirits and Georgian athleticism were sometimes too excessive for Lytton's indoor tastes, yet Garnett's robust good looks, his unabashed conceit, his unselfconscious manner, his matter-of-fact imagination and vivid response to the physical and materialistic side of living, coupled with a strain of modern sensibility, were of a type to which Lytton felt himself inevitably drawn.

(Note that Holroyd does not place a comma after the word 'imagination'. By omitting it he avoids chopping up the sentence into a series of short pieces.)

Exercise 8

1 He wrote requesting an explanation. This letter was followed by a more peremptory demand.

2 The weather, hitherto soft and balmy, has suddenly become cold, wet, and thoroughly wintry.

3 Used properly, with regard for its various functions, the comma is an excellent aid and tool for the writer.

4 Disraeli was an author as well as a politician. He wrote several novels. (Alternatively, a semicolon could be placed after 'politician'.)

5 At last, and just as we were feeling that all hope was gone, we saw a steady gleam of light on the high moor.

The semicolon and the colon

Exercise 9

1 The poem has its own existence apart from us; it was there before us and will endure after us.

2 Modern man has not found substitutes for wheat, barley, oats,

and rice; nor has he domesticated new animals as beasts of burden.

3 Technology sometimes produces ecological mishaps; it also invents the means to deal with them.

4 He had nothing to do with the crime, so we need not interrogate him; nor need we trouble his wife with questions.

Exercise 10

Oliver sat down slowly, his hand held to his brow. He was completely bewildered. What was he to do now? He could try to escape. On the other hand, to stay with these robbers in the hills might be a way of finding out what he wanted to know. If he attempted to escape he would probably be shot in the back. Nothing could be achieved in that way; he would remain.

(It would not be wrong to put a semicolon after 'escape' in l. 2, a comma after 'escape in l. 5, and a full stop after 'way' in l. 6.)

Exercise 11

1 The taste of an adolescent writer is intense but narrow: it is determined by personal needs.

2 There are two forms of impersonality: that which is natural to the more skilful craftsman, and that which is more and more achieved by the maturing artist.

3 To sum up: education must be education for every aspect of life.

4 The Greek thinkers launched mankind into a new search: the search for a system that integrated man with the world.

5 My life had changed radically: I had a regular income, a room of my own, and an enchanting girlfriend.

Exercise 12

There was much to be done: an acre of old garden to be revived; outbuildings to be repaired, cleaned, and returned to use; the whole house to be opened and aired, restored, and made warmly habitable. They felt deeply happy at the prospect of years of honest, exhausting toil lying before them. Mollie had secret plans for a mushroom bed, vines, melons, and peppers. William, true to habit, began to keep a written record of their days. He bought a large, stiff-bound book for the purpose and marked it in sections: kitchen garden, house, outbuildings, paddock, stables, and so on. The great project, dreamed of for so long, had at last begun.

Quotation marks

Exercise 13

1 Smiling, she answered, 'Yes, I shall be there tomorrow'.
2 The Chancellor of the Exchequer, speaking on television, said that nothing would be allowed to weaken his new anti-inflation measures.
3 Do you know that poem by Ted Hughes that begins: 'October is marigold'? (A comma after 'begins' is equally acceptable.)
4 Boltzman said in a lecture: 'Entropy is a measure of physical probability'. (A comma after 'lecture' is equally acceptable.)

Exercise 14

1 His actual words were: 'Tennyson's technical competence is never less than masterly'. (A comma after 'were' is equally acceptable.)
2 'Tell me at once', he said, 'what you mean by that'.
3 Can you remember that speech in *Hamlet* that begins: 'To be or not to be'? (A comma after 'begins' is equally acceptable.)
4 It continues with the words: 'That is the question', doesn't it? (A comma after 'words' is equally acceptable.)

Exercise 15

1 Have you ever watched the TV programme called 'Coronation Street'?
2 When I said that I thought the 'Mona Lisa' was a very great painting, he replied, 'It is all a matter of taste'.
3 I shall have to look up the word 'echelon' in my dictionary.
4 We have designed an electronic mouse and are about to test it to see if it can 'escape' from a maze.
5 Mr Gladstone used to say: 'The photograph cannot lie'. (A comma after 'say' is equally acceptable.)

Dashes, brackets, and hyphens

Exercise 16

1 St Paul has said that the woman – I cite the authorised version of the Bible – is not to usurp authority over the man.
2 There is strong evidence that an exploding star (a supernova) provided the material of the earth.
3 The third question, which is the most searching one by far, will take a little longer to answer.
4 Nearly all flowering plants, which means nearly all the higher plants, are dependent on birds and insects for pollination.
5 Oliver Cromwell – and regicide – ensured that England would be ruled by parliaments, and not by kings.

Comments

1 I am not satisfied with dashes for this parenthesis. Commas will not do; brackets are possible. I would really prefer to recast the sentence:

In the authorised version of the Bible St Paul said that the woman is not to usurp authority over the man.

2 I think that brackets are best for this one, but would not regard either commas or dashes as wrong.
3 Commas will do the work here, so I have used them.
4 Again, commas are satisfactory, but brackets would also be acceptable.
5 One of those instances in which the 'highlighting' effect of dashes is useful.

Exercise 17

1 I think dashes are acceptable in this sentence, although I would prefer commas.
2 This is a clear example of using the dash as an all-purpose punctuation mark. A better version of the sentence is:

They were impressed by a number of items, the old Welsh dresser for one, and thought the whole house had been most cleverly converted and decorated; even noting the careful restoration of the old door locks.

3 The dash is acceptable here, but a semicolon would do the work as well.

4 Once again, the dashes do not offend; but my personal choice would be for commas:

He had said before, and would no doubt say again, that a free market economy could not provide a way out of our economic difficulties.

Exercise 18

1 Shall you be at the end-of-term prize-giving?
2 In the back street they found a little-frequented restaurant.
3 He is an authority on the nineteenth-century English novelists.
4 She has a happy-go-lucky disposition.
5 I'd love to own a fried-fish shop.

Exercise 19

1 This piece of research is a government-financed project.
2 The murder took place in a first-class carriage.
3 My publishing firm has just brought out a paperback about the battlefields of the First World War.
4 This book jacket is so badly torn that I think we shall have to re-cover it.
5 This is a handsome coat of arms belonging to a well-known family.

(I would not count 'coat-of-arms' as wrong. However, the *Shorter Oxford Dictionary* gives it without hyphens, no doubt because no ambiguity results from omitting them.)

6 As a disc-jockey he is well known.

Revision exercise

Exercise 20

The German sociologist, Max Weber, died at about four o'clock on the afternoon of June 14, 1920. The day had been wet, and when Weber's student, Karl Loewenstein, visited the Weber home on the Seestrasse in Munich he found the sick man alone. For a few minutes Loewenstein stayed by the bed, watching the last struggles of his teacher. Then he left. Weber's wife, Marianne, was elsewhere in the house, resting. Shortly after Loewenstein's departure Weber died, unattended and solitary.

Exercise 21

1 Have you a copy of the hymn 'Jerusalem'?
2 What is mind? What is matter? How does one influence the other?
3 During the First World War he was awarded a VC.
4 Mr and Mrs T. Jones walked slowly away from the house in Victoria Street.

Exercise 22

1 Anthropologists used to distinguish between Culture, conceived of as exclusively human, and Nature, which was common to all animals.
2 An experienced anthropologist may, after spending a few days with a primitive society, be able to see exactly how the society's social system works.
3 For the next expedition he bought a small pocket-knife, a billy-can, some bandages and plasters, and three pairs of wool and nylon socks. (Strictly: 'wool-and-nylon'.)
4 This process is new, experimental, slightly risky, and very expensive.

Exercise 23

Already, by the late 1880s, it was obvious that the family was in decline. Now, as the Victorian age tottered towards its exhausted conclusion, and the first grumblings of serious reaction made themselves heard, they looked about and for the first time found themselves out of touch with the rising mood. But within the arid and forbidding precincts of Lancaster Gate everything remained as before, unchanged and unchangeable. Being invited there for the first time was an odd, sometimes even alarming experience, like stepping into another age, perhaps another world.

Exercise 24

1 Classical physics introduced two substances: matter and energy.
2 The theory of relativity disposes of the difficulties of the field theory; it formulates wider mechanical laws; it replaces two conservation laws with one; it changes our concept of time.
3 Do not be afraid of the semicolon; it can be most useful.
4 His purpose was twofold: he would survey the job prospects, and also explore further a part of the country he had always wanted to revisit.

Exercise 25

1 He said that all being well, he would visit her next week.
2 What exactly does the phrase 'turned on' mean?
3 He stated his main theme in the following words: 'This party will not be re-elected until it becomes a united party.'
4 The doctor said to him, 'You must rest for at least a week'.
5 Did he say, 'When is she going?', or 'Where is she going'?
6 Helen asked, 'What did he mean when he whispered, "Tread softly", to you?'

Exercise 26

1 We should be prepared to prohibit a pollutant (an insecticide, for instance) until its long-term effects are known.
2 Man's great memorials – his science, his philosophy, his technology, his architecture, his countryside – are all founded on his attempt to subdue nature.
3 The three attempts at reconciliation (already described in detail on pp. 82–98) did eventually generate some useful discussion.

Exercise 27

1 Tomorrow we shall be meeting the new headmaster.
2 Every cat-owning householder should have a cat-door.
3 My own view is that the Abominable Snowman is non-existent.
4 We shall not succeed without your co-operation.
5 The programme contains both highbrow and lowbrow music.

4 Grammar

Arranging the words

Exercise 1

1 The present administration, now a year old and led by an experienced prime minister, is pursuing a policy of free trade.
2 Some shots were fired at the terrorists' car, which travelled for several miles at high speed before a bullet shattered its rear window.
3 He announced that a discussion about motorbikes would take place in the church vestry.

Exercise 2

1 When I was only a small child, my father took me to the Science Museum.
2 Our money ran out while we were driving across India.
3 This could mean either
The doctor stayed with his patient all morning in spite of other engagements, and then went on his usual round of the wards.
Or:
The doctor stayed with his patient all morning and then, in spite of other engagements, went on his usual round of the wards.
4 An appeal by the secretary of the Community Association for the restoration of the old Guildhall has just been launched.
5 He ran a seminar in the senior common room yesterday on intensive pig-rearing.
Or:
Yesterday he ran a seminar in the senior common room on intensive pig-rearing.

Some common failings

Exercise 3

1 Because of its spectacular black and white plumage the magpie is easily detected in the countryside.

2 He was unable to attend the conference because of (*or* owing to) the heavy floods.
3 ✓
4 Prices have increased because of (*or* owing to) the heavy demand.
5 ✓
6 ✓

Exercise 4
1 The failure of the tests was due to a transcription error in the statistical data we used.
Or:
The reason for the failure of the tests was a transcription error in the statistical data we used.
2 Because of a power failure he had the emergency generator switched on.
3 The reason for the breakdown in law and order was the bad handling of a quite minor incident.
Or:
Law and order broke down because of the bad handling of a quite minor incident.
4 The Bermuda Triangle is an area of sea that is mysteriously dangerous.
5 Acid causes blue litmus paper to turn pink.
Or:
Acid makes blue litmus paper turn pink.

Exercise 5
1 fewer, 2 fewer, 3 less, 4 fewer, 5 less, 6 fewer

Exercise 6
1 We lay out on the sunny hillside all day. (Past tense of intransitive *to lie*.)
2 She was laying out the cards in rows on the table. (Past tense of transitive *to lay*.)
3 If you are feeling faint, you should lie on the bed. (Future tense of intransitive *to lie*.)
(But note that the following is possible:
If you are feeling tired, you should lay yourself down on the bed. (Future of transitive *to lay*.)

4 We left the body where it lay. (Past tense of intransitive *to lie*.)

5 They are laying down new regulations for entry to the chess congress. (Present tense of transitive *to lay*.)

6 The terrified dog lay absolutely still and silent. (Past tense of intransitive *to lie*.)

Prepositions

Exercise 7

I have crossed out:

1 on, through, 2 at, over, 3 to, than, 4 into, about, 5 to, with, 6 to, about, 7 to, by, 8 from, to

Note: *different to* and *different than* were used in older English but *different from* is regarded as correct current usage.

Exercise 8

1 with (*or* from), 2 to, 3 with, 4 at, 5 to, 6 to, 7 with, 8 to

Exercise 9

I have deleted:

1 out, 2 up, 3 into, 4 back, 5 from, 6 again, 7 up

Exercise 10

1 This sentence is not too grotesque as it is, but I think I prefer:

It was the most taxing enterprise he had ever engaged in.

2 There is no good reason why 'down' should be at the end of the sentence. Much better to put:

You have to try to knock down all the ninepins at the end of the gangway.

3 √ (But

To what use will you put it?

is not too pedantic for me.)

4 Without a doubt:

This is the place for used envelopes.

5 √

6 Remember to pick up the ones that have fallen behind the desk.

7 I prefer:

Let us see what it amounts to.

Some debatable points

Exercise 11

1 The work had begun to affect his health seriously.

2 Once again the time has come to sweep up the dead leaves and light the autumn bonfires.

3 The architect has asked us to enlarge the archway slightly.

4 I urge you to acknowledge, humbly and generously, that your political opponents were right on this occasion.

Exercise 12

1 The herd dispersed, kicking their heels and bellowing.

2 What do the public think about this outrage?

3 The Association is concerned with the building standards set by its members.

4 All the audience rose to their feet.

Exercise 13

1 As one reads the narrative of events, one realises that a large body of evidence is being presented for one's consideration.

2 If one studies during the same hours each day, one can acquire good habits and improve one's ability to concentrate.

3 When one applies for a job, one should expect to have one's credentials closely examined.

Rewritten

1 As you read the narrative of events, you realise that a large body of evidence is being presented for your consideration.
Or:
Reading the narrative of events brings the realisation that a large body of evidence is being presented for consideration.

2 If you study during the same hours each day, you can acquire

good work habits and improve your ability to concentrate.
Or:
Studying during the same hours each day helps the acquisition of good work habits and improves the ability to concentrate.
3 When you apply for a job you should expect to have your credentials closely examined.
Or:
Anyone applying for a job should expect to have his or her credentials closely examined.

Common failings again

Exercise 14
1 The imagery, diction, and syntax of each writer were examined.
2 From this study have come several new technical advances.
3 The skilled use of the new machines requires careful training.
4 Evaluation of both teaching and research resources is necessary.
5 The dexterity of his movements is amazing.

Exercise 15
1 who, 2 whom, 3 who, 4 whom, 5 whom, 6 who

Exercise 16
You should have crossed out:

1 yet, 2 if, 3 while, 4 or

Revision exercises

Exercise 17
1 A comfortable chair with an adjustable back is wanted for an old-age pensioner.
2 The rain was soaking him to the skin while he perched on the high slab of rock.
3 A letter of protest was sent in triplicate to the men.
4 The stolen coins were found in a plastic bag by a policeman.

5 She gave a lecture to the Women's Institute on the illegal distribution of cocaine and heroin.

Exercise 18
1 delete 'out', 3 delete 'to', 3 supply 'by', 4 delete 'to', 5 supply 'by', 6 delete 'up'

Exercise 19
1 Because of a fault at the transmitter, they were unable to relay the broadcast.
2 The reason for searching every room is that some dangerous drugs have disappeared.
Or:
Every room is being searched because some dangerous drugs have disappeared.
3 We are not vegetarian, but we are trying to eat fewer meat meals.
4 The poetry course offers more seminars but fewer lectures than the novel course.
5 He lay injured in the ditch all night.
6 We shall lay down several bottles of this fine red wine.

Exercise 20
1 Anxiety and fear had begun slowly and insidiously to warp his powers of judgement.
2 You will have to build up your stamina gradually by swimming a little further each day.
3 Will it be possible to increase the quality of this service substantially and immediately?
4 He began to explain the details of the technique carefully.
Or:
He began carefully to explain the details of the technique.

Exercise 21
1 The service was over, and the congregation were on their way home.
2 The board will let us know its decision tomorrow.
3 The scattered flock of sheep were bleating plaintively.

4 A small committee was elected to choose the books for the American Studies section of the library.

5 The family were unable to agree on a meeting place for the reunion.

Exercise 22
You should have crossed out the following:

1 who, 2 whom, 3 who, 4 who, 5 who

5 Style and diction

Some common failings

Exercise 1

1 *his wife was struck by him*
The use of the passive voice makes this sentence less direct than it might be. It would be better to write:

In the quarrel that followed, he struck his wife.

2 *very fatal final illness*
A fatal illness is one which kills. It cannot therefore be 'very' fatal, and necessarily it is final. So it is enough to say:

We were all shocked to hear of the chairman's fatal illness.

3 *day and age ... grinding to a halt ... wind of change ... heralding the arrival ... climate of opinion*
The sentence is a mass of clichés. I suggest:

Industry is not thriving nowadays and one senses changes that will generate fresh ideas.

4 *remuneration ... subordinate officials ... very considerable proportion ... placed on offer*
The sentence is pompous and longwinded. Why not just:

Compared with similar firms, this one pays its junior employees very well.

5 *proffered the olive branch ... nothing concrete had come out of it*
The mixed metaphors in this sentence produce a ludicrous effect.

You may also feel that 'proffered the olive branch' is something of a cliché. Perhaps the following would be better:

Their political opponents became more friendly, but this made very little difference to the situation.

6 *economically attractive best quality refined chemicals*
Too many descriptive words are packed in front of the noun 'chemicals'. A clearer version is:

These refined, best-quality chemicals will be on sale at a very reasonable price in three months' time.

7 *rose to a steady crescendo*
This is a careless use of 'crescendo', for the word means 'getting louder'. I should think the intended meaning of the sentence was probably:

The noise of the machinery rose to a steady roar.

Exercise 2
1 *leave no stone unturned ... lend a helping hand*
We shall do everything we can to help.
2 *of supreme and paramount importance ... minimum levels*
The most important aim in our education programme is that classes should be kept as small as possible.
3 *speculation was rife ... cool as a cucumber ... took the situation in her stride*
In spite of all the speculation in the senior common room, she remained completely calm and dealt with everything in her usual way.
4 *At the tender mercies ... explore every avenue*
Before our opponents can gain control, let us do all we can to find a way of solving the problem.

Exercise 3
1 *few and far between*
It was extremely difficult to understand his essay because it contained so few commas.
2 *splendid isolation*
Mary Queen of Scots spent many months alone before ...
3 *through thick and thin*

... Horatio remains loyal to the prince throughout.
4 *powers that be*
... until we have official approval.
5 *at a very tender age*
... when very young.

Comment It isn't easy to rewrite a sentence containing a hackneyed phrase or a cliché. However, the attempt to do so is illuminating, for as we struggle to find an apt alternative expression we begin to realise the original force of the now-stale phrase. We see also how such phrases can weaken writing. For instance, when we read 'lived in splendid isolation', we are not sure whether 'splendid' is a precise and essential description of the isolation, or is included merely because it is part of the cliché, or, as is sometimes the case in using clichés, is meant ironically.

Exercise 4
1 The enquiry group noted that some of the information was unreliable.
2 The planners underestimated the cost of the new project and a newly constituted committee has taken over the development of the scheme.
3 Everyone present partook of a huge repast.
4 This method saves a great deal of effort, time, and money.
5 This new young actress gave a charming and intelligent performance.

Diction: misused words

Exercise 5
1 (b) Correct.
  (a) Wrong, because 'chronic' means 'long-lasting'. 'Severe' would be a better word to describe the headache. (But attempts to keep the correct meaning of 'chronic' are failing. Some dictionaries already allow a 'vulgar' meaning: 'bad, intense, severe'.)
2 (a) Correct.

    (b) Wrong, because the verb 'to purport' cannot be used in connection with a person.

3 (b) Correct.
    (a) Wrong, because 'allergic' is a medical term that describes the condition of someone who is sensitive to some substance that is normally harmless. Perhaps it could be argued that this is a *metaphorical* description of a reaction to Wagner's music.

4 (b) Correct.
    (a) Wrong, because a protagonist is the chief person in a drama or story, or the leading person in an event. A protagonist, unlike an antagonist, is not necessarily defending or attacking something.

5 (b) Correct.
    (a) Wrong, because 'crucial' means that which decides between two possibilities. '*Important* for our economy' would have been a better phrase to use.

6 (a) Correct.
    (b) Wrong, because a dilemma is an argument that presents equally unsatisfactory alternatives. A dilemma is generated when we debate whether someone who announces 'I am a liar' has spoken the truth. There is no dilemma over being unable to pay a bill, but simply the unfortunate practical difficulty of obtaining some money.

7 (a) Correct.
    (b) Wrong, because 'facilitate' means to make easy or help forward, but in this sentence it is used as if it meant 'given the services of' or 'assisted by'. It was the research that was facilitated, not the student.

Exercise 6

exotic – introduced from abroad (used of fashions, plants, food, etc.)

valid – sound, well-grounded (particularly of arguments, contracts, documents)

echelon – a formation of troops in which divisions are drawn up in parallel, but with no two on the same alignment

viable – able to live (of organisms)

parameter – a quantity that is constant in a particular case, but varying in different cases (but note that 'parameter' also has other technical meanings in other contexts)

prestigious – practising juggling, sleight of hand, deceptions, illusions, etc. (but probably the popular meaning – 'having prestige' – is now winning)

trauma (pl. traumata) – a morbid bodily condition produced by a wound or violence; an emotional shock

charisma – a talent, favour, gift, or grace

disinterested – impartial and unbiased

Exercise 7

The blanks should be filled as follows:

1 gregarious, 2 attrition, 3 expedient, 4 eminent, 5 expeditious, 6 imminent, 7 expatiate, 8 expiate, 9 contrition, 10 garrulous, 11 explicate, 12 immanent, 13 depreciate, 14 emigrant, 15 factitious, 16 deprecate, 17 immigrant, 18 fictitious

Note: a simple reminder for the uses of 'emigrant' and 'immigrant' is as follows:

an *im*migrant comes *in*
an *em*igrant makes an *ex*it

Ornate writing

Exercise 8
1 The match had to be postponed because of bad weather.
2 We must keep a close watch on this.
3 We shall have to start the conversion of the buildings to homes.
4 Can you tell us the cause of the trouble?
5 Let us start by welcoming our new president.
6 Few applicants understood the job and some were not qualified to do it.

Exercise 9
1 The results were ... *or* The consequences were ...
2 At the moment ... *or* At present ...
3 What are the essentials?

4 I was acting hastily *or* I was acting on impulse.
5 Is it possible?
6 Let's hope they will not prejudge him *or* Let's hope they will not judge him in advance.
7 She continued to complain *or* She still complained.
8 The companies could merge to form a large syndicate.
9 The subject of the talk is our recent economic recovery *or* The talk is about our recent economic recovery.
10 The reason for the delay was his illness *or* The delay was caused by his illness.
11 It seems to me that ... *or* It is apparent to me that ...
12 The majority wanted to accept the offer.

Exercise 10
1 It would be preferable to await the results of this co-operation.
2 We can now offer you part-time work.
3 She was seen driving a blue car down the main street.
4 Be sure to think about it carefully before you act.
5 The new tower block will certainly spoil the view.
6 Mr Thomas had just gone to bed when he remembered that there was a shortage of paperclips at the office.
   Or ... that the office was short of paperclips.

Exercise 11
When buying a second-hand car, you should examine it carefully. In particular, look at the driving seat, because a heavily used car will probably have a badly worn one. Usually, the seller will have touched-up the rust spots on the car's body, so test for rust by running your finger cautiously along the lower rim of the chassis. If you find rust, you may be able to buy at a lower price.

Jargon

Exercise 12
This 83-year-old lady has arthritis, cannot get about and is lonely, confused, and frightened.

(This is the 'translation' offered by a letter-writer to the *Guardian*.)

Exercise 13
I have underlined the following phrases:

1 *incumbent upon me ... operating with a low manpower ceiling*
2 *undertaking a study ... teacher–child communication ... controlled classroom environment*
3 *vegetable protein substitute ... a gravy situation*
4 *developed in recognition of ... socio-economic patterns*

Exercise 14
1 The traffic difficulties in the High Street are increasing.
2 The youths escaped down a rear alley.
3 The chairman's secretary arranged their travel.
4 The council is to make a larger grant to the home improvement programme.
5 Over the past year oil supplies have diminished less rapidly.

Exercise 15
An *acute dilemma* today confronts the *tight-knit little community* of the *sun-baked island* of San Juliano. The *romantic desert island's* main street is *strangely desolate* and an *eerie silence* lies over the *scattering of houses* that *straggle up the steep hillside* behind the *idyllic shoreline.* In San Juliano's tiny *primitive meeting-house* sit ten *grim-faced and silent* men, *their eyes fixed on* the small *intricately carved box* that stands on the *rough wooden table* in the middle of the room.

The italicised phrases are very close to being clichés or hackneyed phrases. The paragraph is written in the style of sensational journalism.

Vocabulary

Exercise 16
1 *promethean* Prometheus was a Titan, said to have created man out of clay. He stands for the whole human enterprise of civilising man, and a promethean task is one of great challenge and size which brings deep suffering.

2 *epicurean*   Epicurus was a Greek philosopher (341–271 BC) who taught that happiness and freedom from care could be gained only by the renunciation of worldly aims, and that men had a right to pursue such happiness. The modern epicurean is someone who cultivates happiness in an enlightened way.

3 *titanic*   The Titans were pre-Olympian gods, the children of Uranus, and often confused with the race of Giants. Anything described as 'titanic' is god-like or giant-like.

4 *procrustean* Procrustes was a legendary robber, owner of a bed on which his victims had to fit, either by being stretched or chopped to size. So 'procrustean' refers to the forcing of individuals to conform to a system.

5 *stoical*   The Stoic school of philosophy was founded by Zeno (335–263 BC). It held that nature is governed by divine reason and that it is man's duty to live in harmony with it. Knowledge of the divine reason enables a man to be indifferent to suffering and to act justly at all times.

6 *protean*   Proteus was a minor sea-god endowed with the gift of prophecy and able to change his shape. So 'protean' means variable and versatile.

7 *draconian*   Draco was an Athenian law-giver who made extremely harsh laws. So 'draconian measures' are very severe ones.

Exercise 17

1 protean, 2 herculean, 3 titanic, 4 epicurean, 5 promethean, 6 stoical, 7 procrustean, 8 draconian

Exercise 18

1 'Oblivious' means forgetful of, *not* ignorant of.

2 'To refute' means to rebut and disprove *by means of argument*, not merely to deny or contradict.

3 'It transpired that' means 'it gradually came out that'. It does not mean 'it happened'.

4 'A discrete entity' is one that is separate and distinct. The word

should not be confused with *discreet*, which means prudent or circumspect about speaking out.

5 'Mitigating circumstances' are circumstances that reduce the severity of a punishment, censure, or disapproval. 'Militate' is sometimes mistakenly used for 'mitigate' and produces an almost opposite meaning.

6 'An alibi' is literally 'an elsewhere', that is, a plea that when an alleged act took place one was elsewhere.

Exercise 19

1 Wrong use of 'mitigate'.
Correction: The information we have just been given is bound to *militate* against his case.

2 √

3 Wrong use of 'oblivious'. I think it is clear that it is not *forgetfulness* but *unawareness* that is meant in the sentence.
Correction: She seemed *unaware* of what was going on around her.
(It is helpful to remember that 'oblivious' should be followed by 'of', not 'to'.)

4 Wrong use of 'refute'.
Correction: I utterly *deny* (or *reject*) your allegations.

5 √

6 Wrong use of 'transpire'.
Correction: Both chess players were in excellent form for what *turned out* to be the last game in the congress.

Revision exercise

Exercise 20

1 The investigators noted that at least one third of the tested rats exhibited stress behaviour.

2 We should certainly say exactly what we are about to do.

3 His support is vital (essential, necessary) to our scheme.

4 Ford's new model has been stringently tested and will soon be on sale all over the country.

5 Three members of the examination board have prepared a specimen paper.

Exercise 21

1 √
2 Wrong.
  Correction: I really detest light romantic novels.
3 √
4 √
5 √

Exercise 22

exotic – introduced from abroad
echelon – a formation of troops in which divisions are drawn up in parallel lines, but with no two on the same alignment
viable – able to live
parameter – a quantity that is constant in a particular case, but varying in different cases
charisma – a talent, favour, gift, or grace
disinterested – impartial and unbiased

Exercise 23

You should have crossed out:

1 immigrate, 2 imminent, 3 contrition, 4 gregarious, 5 expiate

Exercise 24

1 The committee are now discussing recruitment.
2 If a large number enrol we shall be able to reduce the fees.
3 In the 1980s people will probably demand more and better crêches and more maternity and paternity leave.

Exercise 25

1 an ability to adapt to changing circumstances
2 an attitude of reasoned, enduring calm
3 a state of affairs to which one has painfully to adapt
4 stern and rigorous measures
5 a liking for refined pleasures
6 challenging prospects
7 a giant-like immensity
8 great strength

Exercise 26
You should have crossed out the following words:

1 oblivious, 2 alibi, 3 deny, 4 transpired

6 Academic apparatus

Some Latin terms and their abbreviations

Exercise 1

Latin abbreviation	English meaning	Full Latin
e.g.	for example	exempli gratia
i.e.	that is	id est
etc.	and other things	et cetera
viz.	namely	videlicet

Exercise 2
See the chart above.

Exercise 3
1 e.g., 2 viz., 3 i.e., 4 etc.

Exercise 4

Latin abbreviation	English meaning	Full Latin
etc.	and other things	et cetera
i.e.	that is	id est
viz.	namely	videlicet
e.g.	for example	exempli gratia
c.	about, around	circa
v.	see	vide

Latin terms again

Exercise 5
1 A trauma or traumatic experience is something that is not only distressing at the time but also has lasting pathological effects, *that is*, it is a wound which leaves scars. (i.e.)

2 Freud described certain techniques of the ego, *for example*, repression, projection and reaction-formation, as 'defence-mechanisms'. (e.g.)

3 'Anti-psychiatry' became an influential movement in the 1960s and is now under severe critical scrutiny; *see* Cooper D., 'The anti-hospital: an experiment in psychiatry', *New Society*, 11 March 1965, 5, No. 128 (v.)

4 According to Freud, maturation consists in passing through a series of phases which are related to the physical sources of erotic pleasure, *namely*, the oral, anal and phallic. (viz.)

5 Treatment producing fits in patients actually worked best with those patients who had been misdiagnosed, *that is*, those who were not schizophrenic at all. (i.e.)

6 Epidemiology, a method of tracing the sources of an outbreak of a disease, was of course unknown at the time of the scourge of plagues that erupted in Europe *in about* 1390. (c.)

Exercise 6

1 The 'c.' is wrong, as *circa* refers only to a time or date.

2 'i.e.' is wrong. The baker and the girl are *examples* of 'unlikely people', and so e.g. is the correct abbreviation.

3 Correct. The phrase following 'viz.' *specifies* his 'ruling interest'.

4 Correct.

5 Correct. 'Natural selection' is an *example* of 'a basic set of forces'.

6 Correct. The 'i.e.' introduces a *paraphrase* of 'suffer'.

7 'Viz.' is wrong. Doors, dogs, bridges, and cats are *examples* of 'ordinary things', and should be preceded by *e.g.*

Exercise 7

1 viz. (namely), 2 e.g. (for example), 3 i.e. (that is), 4 v. (see), 5 v. (see), 6 i.e. (that is)

Exercise 8

Check by reference to previous charts.

Bibliographies for books and articles

Exercise 9

A bibliography describes books. It gives their authorship, editions, and publication details. When supplied at the end of a piece of scholarly writing the purpose of a bibliography is to enable the interested reader to identify and locate the works the author has referred to or used in producing his own work.

Exercise 11

1 Dimmick, J. D., 'Pragmatism and Principles: a Common-sense View', *Politics for People*, no. 6 (June 1923)
2 Seldon, W. J., *English Country Customs* (Rapier Press, 1966)
3 Diffey, T. J., 'The Idea of Art', *British Journal of Aesthetics*, vol. 17, no. 2 (spring 1977)
4 Miller, J. R., *A Decade of Computer Systems* (Macdonald's, 1980)

References and footnotes in books and articles

Exercise 12

In one of Igor Stravinsky's less charitable conversations he talks of 'a worthy woman who naturally and unfortunately looked irate, like a hen, even when in good humour.'[1] One may quarrel whether hens look irate, maybe peevish would be a better word here, but no one would easily deny that they have an 'expression' which an unfortunate woman may share.

(*footnote*)
[1]Igor Stravinsky and Robert Craft, *Themes and Episodes*, p. 152.

(*bibliography*)
Stravinsky, I., and Craft, Robert, *Themes and Episodes* (New York, 1966)

Exercise 13

Although religious belief is in decline, there are still many people who experience a deep revulsion at the thought of genetic tampering. The origins of this revulsion are questioned in an article by Edward Shils. Is it, he asks, simply a vestigial feeling left over from earlier beliefs?[1]

(*footnote*)
[1]Edward Shils, 'The Sanctity of Life', p. 43.

(*bibliography*)
Shils, Edward, 'The Sanctity of Life', *Encounter*, vol. xxviii, no. 1 (January 1967)

Exercise 14
1 Manuel, F. (1968), *A Portrait of Isaac Newton*, Harvard University Press, pp. 9, 10.
2 Nagel, E. (1961), *The Structure of Science*, London, Routledge.
3 Weber, Max (1957), *The Methodology of the Social Sciences*, Chicago, Free Press.

(Note that this style of bibliographic description usually ends the description with a stop.)

A method for essays; abbreviations; some Latin phrases

Exercise 15
1 [1]J. Cott, *Stockhausen: Conversations with the Composer* (Pan Books, 1974), p. 47.
2 [2]E. Ashby, 'Towards an Environmental Ethic', *Nature*, 262 (1976), pp. 84, 85.
3 [3]S. Sweig, *Beware of Pity*, trans. P. and T. Blewitt (Cassell, 1940)

Exercise 16

MS., MSS	manuscript, manuscripts
p., pp.	page, pages
l., ll.	line, lines
f., ff.	and the following page, and the following pages
v. (vide)	see
ch., chs	chapter, chapters

vol., vols	volume, volumes
ed., eds	editor, editors
fig., figs	figure, figures
trans., tr.	translated by
et al.	(*et alii*) and others
no., nos	number, numbers
para., paras	paragraph, paragraphs
cp.	compare

Exercise 17

1 This piece of research was not completed because *page* 102 of the *manuscript* was missing and no further *manuscripts* could be traced. (p. 102, MS., MSS)

2 In *Critical Appraisals*, *volume* 1, *chapters* 4 and 5 are devoted to a rebuttal of the objections made by Cooper and James. (vol., chs)

3 The first two *paragraphs* of *page* 10 relate to *figures* 1, 2 and 3; *lines 12–16* of the third *paragraph* refer only to *figure* 4. (paras, p., figs, ll. 12–16, para., fig.)

4 For a fuller discussion, *see* H. Leach and H. J. Crane, *editors*, *Readings in Social Psychology* (Hyam's Press, 1980), *volume* 4, *pages* 42–79, *page* 83, *and those following it*. (v., eds, vol., pp., p., ff.)

Exercise 18

1 to infinity, 2 in itself, 3 as, 4 so, thus, 5 the reverse, 6 for this particular purpose

Sic is generally used to draw attention to a misprint or absurdity in a quoted or reported passage. It lets the reader know that the writer is aware of and wishes to point out the incorrectness or absurdity of the quoted words. It is often placed in square brackets immediately following the mistake or peculiarity it indicates.

Revision exercises

Exercise 19

1 i.e. (that is), 2 viz. (namely), 3 e.g. (for example), 4 etc. (and other things)

Exercise 20

1 reference footnote, 2 bibliographic entry, 3 reference footnote

Exercise 21

1 *Lines* 3–15 on *page* 22 comprise a passage taken from a *manuscript, translated by* Edward Bayer, which is discussed in full in *chapter* 5, *page* 82 *and the following pages* (ll., p., MS., trans., ch., p., ff.)

2 A survey conducted by Friedson *and others* has been reported in three *volumes, edited by* R. V. Singer. (et al., vols, ed.)

3 Dawson's theory is mentioned on *pages* 30, 31 of *Witchcraft, edited by* P. R. Jones (LMP, 1960), and also in the closing *paragraphs* of *chapter* 10 *in the same work.* (pp., ed., paras, ch., op. cit.)

4 *Compare figure* 1 on *page* 2 with *figures* 8 and 9 on *pages* 7, 8. (cp., fig., p., figs, pp.)

5 Sonata *number* 10 in the *manuscript* has *four* movements; *numbers* 11 and 12 have only *three.* (no., MS., 4, nos, 3)

Exercise 22

1 Thomas Szasz, *Ideology and Insanity* (Penguin, 1974), p. 80.

2 Maurice Wiles, 'Myth in Theology', *The Myth of God Incarnate,* ed. John Hick (SCM Press Ltd, 1977).

3 T. S. Eliot, *Introducing James Joyce* (Faber and Faber, 1972).

Exercise 23

1 *sic*, 2 *per se*, 3 *vice versa*, 4 *qua*, 5 *ad hoc*

Exercise 24

1 [1]pages, [2]in the same place, page, and the following pages, [3]*circa* = around, about, [4]*vide* = see, chapter, [5]compare, chapter.

2 para., op. cit., etc., fig., et al., ll., Esq.

3 The purpose of a bibliographic description is to enable the reader to identify the *work* quoted or used; that of a reference footnote to locate precisely the *part* of a work referred to.

7 Making notes

Your answers to the exercises in this chapter will undoubtedly vary from mine, especially in their wording and numbering systems. That doesn't matter; it certainly doesn't mean that your answers are wrong or are inferior to mine. The point of the exercises is to give you practice in using a range of note-taking techniques, and scope for developing ideas of your own about abbreviating, layout, and so on.

Techniques and materials

Exercise 1

1   POLITICS   Aristotle
                              Book One
    Chapter 1
2   ENGLISH WORKS (Molesworth edn) Thomas Hobbes
              Volume One: Elements of Philosophy
    Chapter 1: 'Of Philosophy'
3   COTTAGE ECONOMY   William Cobbett
    Introduction
4   AESTHETICS AND LANGUAGE ed. William Elton
        1. 'The Function of Philosophical Aesthetics' W. B. Gallie

Exercise 2

1 American settlers – two methods of preserving smoked ham:
    (1) *lime whitewash* linen cloths sewn round hams, then wash 4/5
        times drying in sun between times;
    (2) lay and cover hams in fine *wood ash* in wooden chest.
2 *In the sea*
    (a) *Above* substratum:
        fishes, opossum shrimps, cuttlefishes.
    (b) *On* substratum:
        starfishes, crabs, lobsters.
    (c) *Beneath* substratum:
        burrowing worms, brittle-starfishes, heart-urchins, crabs.

Brevity

Exercise 3

1 State of science c. 1798: v. Sir H. Hartley, *Humphrey Davy*, pp. 1–8.
2 cp. pt I, fig. 3 with pt II, figs 8, 9.
3 Were C19 politics *really* 'buoyantly optimistic'?
4 Purple Emperor > White Admiral > Comma.

Exercise 4

1 1st scientific study of yoghurt made early C19 by Ilya Metchnikoff, Lister Inst., Paris.
2 *Revealed theology* = based on revelation.
   Natural theology = reasoning about nat. universe.
3 Sir Arthur Conan Doyle, b. Edinburgh 1859, w. known through Sherlock Holmes bks. Wide influence on criminology, e.g. Chinese, Egyptian police used bks as training manuals; FBI adopted detection methods.
4 T. S. Eliot:
   Family *primary* transmitter of culture, but not only one; others are universities, craftsmen, organisations, societies.

Exercise 5

1 When lecturing, first *state point* briefly, using *key term*. *Display* key term, then *restate point* in new way to provide second opportunity to understand.

   Or:

   Lecturing
   (a) State point briefly
   (b) Display its key term
   (c) Restate point in new way
2 No Art, only artists, who once painted cave walls; now do posters for Underground. All artistic activities may be called art, *but* the word means many things. NB: *no Art* with *capital A*.

More techniques

Exercise 6
Here is just one way of arranging the material diagrammatically:

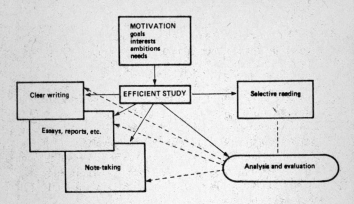

Exercise 7
1 Laymen tend to use 'demand' to mean a quantity of goods bought monthly or yearly. But for the economist it means the factors that *determine* buying: it is the relationship between what *influences* buying and the *amounts* bought.
2 Soil appears simple and harmless but is actually a very complex substance. Good soil is full of life: one teaspoonful contains millions of various bacteria, algae, microscopic animals, mycelium of fungi, and viruses.

Exercise 8
I suggest the *artists' names* for the subject-headings of the cards. For the sub-headings you could have:

Artists' dates, city of residence, etc.
Title/subject of painting (with dimensions, location, medium)
Virgin's robes – colours, etc.
Blue – general use in the paintings

Notes of arguments

Exercise 9

1 Coal is the basis of England's greatness.
   ∴ If there is no coal, there will be no greatness.
2 Some mentally ill people:
   (a) may harm or kill others;
   (b) may harm or kill themselves.
   ∴ They should be compulsorily confined to hospital.

Exercise 10

1 Wearing school uniform:
   conceals financial and social differences;
   disposes of problem of making school rules about clothes;
   makes life easier for parents;
   engenders school spirit.
   ∴ All schools should have some sort of uniform.
2 Beautiful art is produced only in b. surroundings.
   ∴ If workmen have no beauty in surroundings, they will not produce b. things.

Taking relevant notes

Exercise 11

1 Introduction to *Leviathan* (p. 10) C. B. Macpherson
   Hobbes thought he was 1st to make politics a *science with infallible rules*: a bold claim and bold science.
2 Open University correspondence unit
   H.'s greatness was in his *method*. Extended concepts in C17 *physical sciences* to apply to human nature and *civil society*. Aimed at 'complete and incontestable knowledge' through method.

   Method derived from geometry, which uses deductive reasoning to reach conclusions that *cannot be otherwise*. Result a *science* of politics because, in C17, 'science' meant knowledge arrived at by deductive reasoning.

3 *Hobbes* (p. 20) D. D. Raphael

Geometry *itself* not applicable to human behaviour, but its method of *reasoning* necessary for any *scientific* study. (See meaning of 'science' above.)

4 'Thomas Hobbes' (pp. 305, 307, 309) John Aubrey

H. 40 when he first read Euclid. 'This made him in love with geometry.'

5 *Hobbes* (p. 74) R. S. Peters

H. *right* to claim originality. He tried to explain *human behaviour* in the same way as *movements of bodies* are explained. This was new in Ⓒ17.

Revision exercises

Exercise 12

1 Ireland 1st invaded 1169; beg. 1845, still source of anxiety for Eng.

2 Joseph Conrad, *Chance*, imp. novel, 1st pub. Methuen, 1913.

3 Prob. vegetation on Mars ∴ seasonal colour changes, spectroscopic evidence.

4 Bass recorder > tenor > alto > treble > sopranino (smallest).

Exercise 13

1 1778–83 Lavoisier concentrated on thermochemistry. With Laplace invented ice calorimeter to determine heats of reaction and combustion.

2 Research: first, a question; second, attempt answer – 'formulate hypothesis'.

3 Defoe our 1st gt novelist ∴ 1st gt journalist; 1st gt journalist ∴ < born into *life*.

4 Each has active and passive vocab. Active: words *used*. Passive: words *understood*.

Exercise 14

Human *character* tells us what kind of government is right for human beings. Nature made us beings who cannot *alone* supply our individual wants, thereby ensuring that we would congregate in societies and so be the social animals she intended.

Exercise 15

We find it fun to wander down a twisting lane.
Children prefer rubbish dumps, derelict buildings, to neat playgrounds.
∴ It is against human nature to live in a tidily geometrical environment.

Exercise 16

Introduction to *Rights of Man* (pp. v, vi, xii, xiii) Arthur Seldon

1737 Thomas Paine b. Thetford, son of Quaker stay-maker
1774 To America; ed. *Pennsylvania Magazine*
1776 Tract, *Common Sense* pub. (inspired moves to Declaration of Independence, July 1776, drafted by Jefferson, P.'s friend). Appointed sec. of commission to Indians; then sec. to Congressional Comm. Foreign Affairs
1787 Returned Europe
1791 Pub. Pt I, *Rights of Man* in reply to Burke's *Reflections*
1792 Indicted for treason because of *Rights of Man*, Pt II.
1802 To America, but now unpopular
1809 Died in N. York
1819 Body taken to England by William Cobbett

8 Essay writing

Basic form

Exercise 1

You should not expect your basic forms to be just like mine. There is no absolutely 'right' form for an essay. What is important is that you try to derive a broad pattern that can accommodate an answer to the question. Constructing a basic form starts you thinking about the precise meaning of a question.

1	'Do we lead softer lives than our grandparents did?'	
Our lives	*Their lives*	*Which softer, and why*
General verdict and summing up		

2 'Does scientific advance erode or strengthen religious belief?'		
Examples of sc. advances	*Does it erode r.b.?*	*Does it strengthen r.b.?*
General conclusions, remarks, etc.		

3	'Is pride much the same as vanity?'
Pride is: *Vanity is:* *(attempt broad definitions)*	
Differences	*Similarities*
Conclusion and comments	

Notice that at this stage all the emphasis is on *form* rather than on content. You do not need to know much, or have thought in detail, about the content of an essay in order to devise a basic form for it.

Exercise 2

1 What *arguments* are there *against* the contention that no one today can be regarded as *well educated* without a knowledge of *general science*?

2 *Contrast and compare* the *benefits* of city life with those of country life.

3 If you had to choose, which would you take: a *contented* life as a *nonentity* or a *turbulent* life of *fame*? Give *reasons* for your choice.

Once again, your answers may vary from mine. Perhaps you underlined 'contention' in 1, 'city' and 'country' in 2, and 'choice' in 3. So why didn't I? Simply because it did not seem to me that those words, in the context of these particular questions, needed special consideration. I underlined the words that told me what I must do in writing my answer, and words that would need discussion or definition.

The essay plan

Exercise 3

Discuss – investigate or examine by argument; debate, giving reasons; examine the implications of

Explain – make plain; give reasons for; account for

Argue for – bring forward reasons in support of

Analyse – separate and distinguish elements of; take to pieces

Summarise – set out main points of a matter in a concise and orderly way

Evaluate – work out the value of; assess merit of

Define – state the essential nature of; characterise and give the meaning of

Critically examine – carefully investigate and estimate; make reasoned judgements about

Outline – state main features and general principles of a subject, emphasising structure

Justify – give reasoned argument for decisions or claims, meeting objections

Describe – give detailed or graphic account of

217

Contrast and compare – point out differences and similarities

Exercise 4
'*Discuss* the claim that science and technology *do more* than the arts
to make a society *civilised*'

Definition: A civilised society is one that ...	
Science and technology provide	*The arts provide*
Ease of living – domestic life health comfort leisure	Enrichment of – social life family life leisure
Mobility/com- munication – of goods persons ideas and information	Broadening of sympathies sensibility understanding
Materials/skills equipment tools facilities buildings	Counteractions to dehumanising effects of technology and science A *spur* to technology?
Discussion: Much hangs on what is meant by 'civilised'. Science and technology *need* the arts, and *vice versa*? Would the arts flourish without the easement provided by S. and T?	

Probably our plans are not very similar, but I hope you agree with
me that a discussion of what a *civilised* society is like must be an
important element in the essay.

Content for the plan

Exercise 5

For abolition of breakfast	Against abolition of breakfast	Assessments
2.3 No washing-up in morning	1.2 General health bound to suffer	4.2 Abolition almost certainly bad for children, elderly, and 'physical' workers
1.2 General health better?	1.1 Bad for slimming because huge lunch needed	
2.5 Could get up later	2.2 Loss of family occasion	4.1 Health/diet arguments against abolition are mostly strong ones
2.4 Would suit working parents	1.5 Bad for 'physical' workers	
2.1 Time to get up properly	3.1 Bad for grocers	4.4 Might be good for *some* to rearrange whole eating pattern: 'brunch' at eleven a.m., early evening meal
2.2 Does away with family breakfast squabbles	2.1 No incentive to get up	
1.1 Aid to slimming	1.4 Bad for children and elderly	
	3.2 Bad for cereal growers and manufacturers	4.3 Abolition might be good for some adults and overweights whose lifestyle it suited
1 = health and diet 2 = social and practical 3 = economic and other 4 = assessments	1.6 Bad for everyone in cold weather	

Six recommendations for writing an essay

Exercise 6
1 Read the question carefully to see exactly what it means and what it requires you to do. Devise a basic form for the essay, noting key words in the question.
2 Develop an outline plan that will deal systematically with the question.
3 Assemble the books and notes you will need to use when writing the essay.
4 Jot down the main points that you think should be included in the essay and fit them into the essay plan.
5 Write a short opening paragraph to the essay and/or a short paragraph embodying your main idea, conclusion, argument, or claim.
6 Refer back to the question to check that you are actually doing what it asks of you.

Exercise 7
To my mind, that first paragraph will not do. 'Commence' is a rather pompous word, redolent of civic ceremonies. 'Important' and 'salient' are so alike in meaning in this particular context that it is pointless to use both of them. Look up 'salient' in your dictionary if you don't know exactly what it means.

A better opening might be:

'The most important features of the Italian renaissance were ...'

The second sentence of the first paragraph is little more than an excuse for scanty preparation. I would be inclined to excise the whole of the first paragraph and begin the essay with the second one, which provides a direct and interesting opening.

Beginnings, endings, and paragraphs

Exercise 8
My order of preference is: One, Three, Two.

One
A short, clear opening which manages in just one sentence to

suggest the complexity of the term 'culture' and to indicate the direction and scope of the essay. An obvious way to continue is to discuss the 'different associations' that the term has when applied to individuals, groups, and societies.

Three

A punchy opening that creates immediate interest and takes the reader directly into a consideration of one particular connotation of the term 'culture'.

Two

A poor opening, for the following reasons. First, it is *vague*. Second, it does not directly confront what is at issue in the question. Third, it *assumes* that the products of civilisation are 'music, art, and literature'. It is just possible that this opening could be redeemed by subsequent paragraphs.

Exercise 9

1 The paragraph is not a unity. At first it looks as though it is discussing educational opportunities in Britain, but then it wanders away into general complaints about the unfair advantages of being rich. There is no main idea, or connected set of ideas. Even if a new paragraph were started at 'Wealth has always ...', the passage would still lack a strong connexion between the paragraphs.

2 Thoroughly good throughout. It has a main idea – 'The writer I like' – and this idea is developed in a coherent way. Almost a mini-essay in its completeness.

3 It isn't easy to detect what is wrong in this one. The two opening sentences look promising, but the first sentence of the second paragraph seems incongruous. It would be better if it were tacked on to the first paragraph so that the second paragraph begins with 'Primitive crafts ...'. This would give two distinct paragraphs, related to both the title and each other by the broad historical movement from the primitive to the nineteenth century.

4 This paragraph loses coherence after the first two sentences. The third sentence takes a new direction which does not appear to have any strong relationship either to the first two sentences or to the title.

Referring back; revision exercises

Exercise 10

1 I am inclined to say that nothing in this paragraph relates *directly* to the essay question. The opening sentence looks at first as if it is going to be very positive, but then it sheers away from the issue. The second sentence comes nowhere near to discussing the definition in the title. The third sentence tells us how unhappiness can arise, but not what it is or is not.

2 A difficult one. Only with the opening sentence of the second paragraph do we begin to see that there is some point to what looked like a rather vague and off-the-point first paragraph. A much pithier opening could be achieved by amalgamating the ideas of the two paragraphs thus:

If astrology were a science, would all those professedly rational people who so furtively consult their 'stars' in the weekly magazines be quite so anxious to conceal their interest?

Exercise 11

'Read the question carefully.'

Exercise 12

'Whether it is long or short, a paragraph develops one main idea.'

Exercise 13

Here is my attempt. You may like to criticise it for structure, unity and relevance.

If breakfast were abolished we would be saved the preparation, serving, consuming, and clearing of our most complicated and squalor-producing meal. However, a great deal has to be taken into consideration before deciding to abolish it. Breakfast is important to some people for reasons of health and diet; to others for social, family, and psychological reasons; to others yet, because their livelihood depends in one way or another on the manufacture, distribution or sale of breakfast foods.

Exercise 14

Here is my suggestion for a basic form:

Favourite novel is:

What I *like* so much	*Analysis* of likings	Examples from novel

Index